Business Economics

Business Economics

Volume -I

Venugopal
K. Ramachandra

PUBLISHING FOR ONE WORLD

NEW AGE INTERNATIONAL (P) LIMITED, PUBLISHERS
(formerly Wiley Eastern Limited)
New Delhi • Bangalore • Chennai • Cochin • Guwahati • Hyderabad
Jalandhar • Kolkata • Lucknow • Mumbai • Ranchi
Visit us at www.newagepublishers.com

Published by New Age International (P) Ltd., Publishers
First Edition : 2006

ISBN : 81-224-1941-0

Rs. 95.00

C-06-07-873

Printed in India at Ramaprintograph, Delhi.
Typeset at Monu Printers, Delhi.

PUBLISHING FOR ONE WORLD

NEW AGE INTERNATIONAL (P) LIMITED, PUBLISHERS
(formerly Wiley Eastern Limited)
4835/24, Ansari Road, Daryaganj, New Delhi - 110002
Visit us at **www.newagepublishers.com**

PREFACE

Undeniably, there is growing competition now among business houses more than at any point of time. The competition is not merely local or national, but it has become global. This is an era of intense competition sparked off by Knowledge Economics, Outsourcing of business and around the globe companies try to prove their one-up-manship through sophistication, diversification, outsourcing, upgradation, etc. Business standards and the way of doing things are fast changing and now people are ready to relearn and redefine trade for success and global success to put it more aptly.

The dismantling of conservative trade practices, licenses, permits and global agreements on free trade. Crumbling political, trade and legal barriers for mutual co-operation have made it possible for any company to set up shop in any part of the globe. Free trade agreements and technological revolution have made corporate houses to face global challenges. The legal recognition of transactions done through 'electronic' data, interchange assumes importance of electronic Commerce (*e*-Commerce). The concept of global village has become true with the shrinking of space, time and growing competition.

With globalisation; there is a smooth flow of goods, services, capital, technology, professionalism and human resources from one part of the globe to another. The shrinking distances have brought people closer and cross-cultural relationship is established aided by the demolition of language barriers.

Companies today are under pressure and many Indian companies aspire to become MNCs. CEOs are engaged in building business empires as the restrictions have given way to co-operation, global competition and technology addition. Indian has robust opportunity to develop the economy through corporate houses as the Confederation of Indian Industry (CII) has a strong band of 4800 members. The aspirations to increase the share in the global trade which stands at a mere 0.7 percent has to be improved through competition and co-operation.

It is important to learn as to what 'Business', 'Economics' and 'Business Economics' is all about. Further it is important to know as to what the objectives of these terms are; how significant they are in the economic activities of any country, how to use scarce resources effectively to increase productivity. How to bring about the welfare of the consumers in the society by providing goods and services at reasonable prices in the context of global competition are also very pertinent questions in the realm of Business Economics. We shall also discuss the nuances of economic concepts and principles that help business houses to survive, to compete and to take quality decisions.

Every chapter in the text book encompasses rich, relevant, contemporary living and meaningful examples. The subtopics are arranged meticulously. After perusing through the competitive books, the authors appropriately have included the unique features of the relevant chapters which are uncovered in other books. The skill development aspects in the book will certainly augment students practical orientation with ample scope for creativity, innovativeness and demystifying of mystic concepts such as cost and its behaviour, demand, price, supply equilibrium and forecasting techniques. The book is student friendly and worth readable and has value for money for sure. We expect constructive criticism and suggestions from our most valued student and teaching community.

AUTHORS

ACKNOWLEDGEMENTS

The authors wish to express their gratitude to the following personalities for their valuable guidance, encouragement, support, hospitality and benediction —

1. Dr. K. Ashwathappa, Director, Canara Bank School of Management Studies, Bangalore University, Bangalore.
2. Dr. B.C. Sanjeevaiah, Dean and Chairman, Department of Commerce, Bangalore University, Bangalore.
3. Dr. D.K. Murthy, Reader in Commerce, Bangalore University, Bangalore.
4. Prof. B.L. Bhagyalakshmi, Principal, Government R.C. College of Commerce and Management, Bangalore.
5. Dr. L.N. Sheshagiri, Department of English, Maharani's Arts and Commerce College, Bangalore.

CONTENTS

CHAPTER

1

INTRODUCTION

CHAPTER OUTLINE	LEARNING OBJECTIVES
What is business ? — An overview What is economics ? — An overview What is business economics? — Meaning of business economics — Scope of business economics — Definitions — Features — Objectives — Difference between business economics and economics — Business operations and business environment — The role of economist — Responsibilities of a business economist — Uses of business economics	After reading this chapter, you should be able to : 1. Understand the nature and scope of business 2. Define business, economics and business economics 3. Shortlist characteristics and objectives of business economics 4. Differentiate between business operations and business environment 5. Describe the role and responsibilities of a business economist 6. Identify the uses of business economics.

It is pertinent and appropriate to ask questions as to why only some companies like HLL, RIL, Wipro, SAIL, HDFC, ONGC, Dr. Reddy's Lab, Satyam computer, Smithline and Beccham are successful Whereas WIDIA, NGEF, SKF, Kirloskar are not. There are many factors which contribute either to the success or failure of a company. Some of the very important factors that contribute to survival and success of a company are; timely and accurate decision-making, taking stock of the business environment, forecasting and monitoring the environment, people management, redefining the corporate goals in accordance with dynamic situations, business mapping, product addition - deletion, optimum output, government policies, these and many more are worthy of careful and cautious observation for a businessman to script his success story.

India has no dearth of such people, who have scripted their success stories. With perseverance and right decisions at right time people like J.R.D. Tata, Lalbhai, Chidambaram, Birla, Rahul Bajaj, Aditi Godrej, Deepak parekh, Krishna Murthy, late Dhirubai Ambani, Anil and Mukesh Ambani, Narayana Murthy, Azim Premji, Anji Reddy, Shivanader, have steered their way to the peak of cliff.

Business may be understood as the organised efforts of enterprises to supply the consumers with goods and services for fulfilling the needs and wants. They may earn profit or incur loss and they have to do this within the framework of law. All businesses share the same purpose that is to earn profits. The purpose of business goes beyond earning profit. It is an important institution in society be it for the supply of goods and services, creation of job opportunities, offer of better quality of life; or contributing to the economic growth of the country and putting it on the global map, the role of business is crucial. Society needs business and vice-versa.

MEANING OF BUSINESS

Business refers to all the activities concerned with production, manufacturing, lending, selling, leasing and the like, for earning profit. In the process of executing business activities the businessmen/executives in the organisation have to take various business decisions. In the process of taking various business decisions the businessmen should study the behaviour of economic laws or principles or theory. These economic laws or the principles of economics influence the business of the organisation in the process of earning/maximizing profits.

ECONOMICS

If the resources are abundant and the needs and wants are minimal, there is no need to study the economics. The subject economics came into being because there are limitless needs and wants and scarce resources it calls for choice to manage the wants and needs with the scarce resources. The problem of allocation of scarce resources gave birth to a subject called economics. It is a science of choice and it is a 150-year-old discipline. Noted economists described 'Economics' as a study of household management. Adam Smith viewed it as study of 'Wealth", Alfered Marshall as 'Welfare', Robins as use of scares resources Paul A. Samuelson as growth definition. All said and done, the discipline Economics is the study of choice, and involves decision making in every aspect of business and human activity.

The commonly used definition of Economics is the study of the use of limited resources for the achievement of alternative ends[1]. More specifically, Economics may be defined

[1] James M. Henderson and Richard E. Quandt, "Microeconomic Theory- A Mathematical Approach, Tata McGraw-Hill, New Delhi, p-1

as a social science, which covers the actions of individuals and groups of individuals in the processes of producing, exchanging, and consuming goods and services.[2]

Hence the application of the economics in day to day business starting from the establishing the business organisation to production, distribution, sales, after sales and also the keeping the customer relationship for future market is necessary. Hence business economics developed as a branch of economics.

BUSINESS ECONOMICS

Business economics is a special branch of economics. It evolved to bridge the gap between abstract theory and business practice. Business economics deals with the use of economic concepts and principles for decision making in a business organisation. The term managerial economics is interchangeably used in place of business economics.[3]

It is the application of economic theories, concepts, doctrines, principles, and roles to decision-making processes in business. It is a confluence of economic principles and business decisions. Economics spreads, pervades the business decision-making willy-nilly, and removes catharsis of ineffective decision-making and business losses considerably.

Business economics is like an umbrella, which provides safe haven to businessmen. If a businessman treads the corridors of business without the support of business economics, he treads on a slippery lane and come to grief. Economic principles provide comprehensive cover under difficult and smooth conditions of business houses.

Maruti-Suzuki, a joint venture car making automobile company steers ahead inspite of intense competition in the small-car segment in India, because of its pricing strategy and target market. The company effectively availed pricing strategies—a concept given by economics.

In India under slack and recession period, many IT companies recklessly retrenched the employees, but companies like Infosys did not do that because of its strong tenet that success of business solely depends on its people. Infosys strongly believed and adhered to the concept that every slack period is followed by progression period, borrowing the concept from economics that is the phase of trade or business cycle.

ITC jumped to FMCG sector of biscuits making, readymix foods, garments, etc. guided by diversification. Which is again the concept of economic product mix. We have many number of cases and incidents where, business is guided by economic principles for decision - making and future planning through forecasting and SWOT analysis in the context of ever changing business environment.

MEANING OF BUSINESS ECONOMICS

Business economics is an application of economic theory to the business practice for decision making and forward planning.

---

[2]Op.cit., p.1.

[3] Milton H. Spencer and Louis Siegelman, "Managerial Economics", Richard D. Irwin, Inc., Homewood, Illinois, 1959, p.1.

Decision-making refers to the process of selecting one action out of several alternative actions. For example if a manufacturer of a product, wants to buy raw materials in the market the production department call for tenders or quotations. When quotations are received a comparative statement of the quotations has to be prepared and one customer has to be selected from the available customers by considering the reliability, quality of the raw material, price etc. This process of selecting one out of several customers is called decision making in business. In simple, when you go to a shop to purchase pen, you will find several brands of pens in the shop. Out of these brands you will select one based on your preference. This process is called Decision-Making.

Forward planning is a process of thinking in advance or it implies planning in advance for the future. In any business organisation the actions of tomorrow are thought in advance. For example the business organisation has to think in advance, what would be the sales in the next month? What is the extent of stock of the goods that should be possesed? Does the manufacture of the product is further required? What would be the sales promotion strategy in the near future to increase sales etc is thought in advance for the successful business.

DEFINITIONS

There are various definitions on business economics, among them the following are worth to understand.

According to **McNair and Meriam** "Managerial economics consists of the use of economic modes of thought to analyse business situations".[4]

Spencer and siegelman have defined business economics as "the integration of economic theory with business practice for the purpose of facilitating decision-making and forward planning by management".[5]

According to **Prof. Joel Dean**- "the purpose of managerial economics is to show how economics analysis can be used in formulating business policies". [6]

Prof. Norman F. Dufty has defined Business Economics as "a body of theory which can be of considerable assistance to the businessman in his decision making."

Brigham and Pappas believe that managerial economics is "the application of economic theory and methodology to business administration practice."

From the above definitions we can draw the following conclusions

1. Business economics is a branch of economics.
2. The term business economics can be used in place of managerial economics/Industrial economies.
3. The principles or theory of economics is applied to solve the problems of business organisation through decision making and forward planning.

---

[4] Malcolm P. McNair and Richard S. Meriam, "Problems in Business Economics" McGraw-Hill Book Co., Inc., New York and London, 1941. P.v) preface)

[5] Milton H. Spencer and Louis Siegelman, "Managerial Economics", Richard D. Irwin, Inc., Homewood, Illinois, 1959, p.1.

[6] Dean, Joel, "Managerial Economics", Prentice–Hall of India, New Delhi, eg. 1977.

4. The business economics integrates economic theory with business practice

Features or Characteristics of Business Economics

The following are the chief characteristic of business economics.

Characteristics of Business Economics

1. Micro economics
2. Realistic business economics
3. Pragmatic science
4. Normative science
5. Body of economics concepts & principles
6. Studies only the theory of profits
7. Science of decision making and forward planning
8. It uses the services of other sister subjects.

1. Business economics studies the problems of individual business or firm hence it is **micro economics** in character.
2. Business economics is **realistic** because it studies the real business problems like demand determination, demand forecasting, pricing of a product, type of competition their price determination etc.
3. It is **pragmatic** science and highlights practical application of various economic theories like demand theory in determining the demand, cost theory to determine cost, price theory to determine price etc., to solve business problems.
4. Business economics is normative science rather than positive science. **Positive science** deals with things as they are. It explains their causes and effects. For example it studies what factor determines the rate of interest? What are the forces, which influence the determination of the rate of interest? It refuses to pass value judgements like whether these forces are fair or not. **Normative science** studies the things, as they ought to be or should be and hence involves value judgements. It studies what constitutes a fair rate of interest? Any enquiry into this shall immediately become a normative enquiry because it considers the ethical value. Hence business economics is prescriptive rather than descriptive study.
5. Business economics largely uses that **body of economic concepts and principles** to solve the business problems.
6. As a part of the theory of distribution, it studies only the theory of profits.
7. It is a **science of decision making** and **forward planning.** Business economist will collect the information in a systematic manner and analyse the information to take decisions.
8. It uses the services of many other sister subjects like statistics, mathematics, operation research, Accounting, psychology etc.

Objectives of Business Economics

The following are the objectives

Objectives of Business Economics
1. Integration of economic theory with business practice
2. Avoiding abstract discussion
3. Practical application of economics concepts to business problems
4. Employing modern tools to solve business problems
5. Optimum use of scarce resources
6. All round development of the firm

1. Business economics aims at integration of economic theory with business practice.
2. Business economics aims at avoiding abstract discussion.
3. It aims at practical application of economic concepts and principles to solve business problems.
4. It employs most modern instruments and tools to solve business problems.
5. It aims at the optimum use of scarce resources of a firm.
6. It aims at all round development of the firm.

Differences between Business Economics and Economics

There are several differences between Business Economics and Economics. The following are some basic differences.

1. Business economics is an application of economic principles to the business management to solve the problems of the business. Whereas economics is a body of economic principles itself.
2. Business economics is micro in character. Whereas economics is both micro and macro in character.
3. Business economics study the problems of the individual firm and has nothing to do with the problems of the individuals, whereas economics deals with the problems of the firm and the individuals.
4. In business economics only profit theory is used, whereas in economics all the theories of factors of productions are used.
5. Economic theory hypothesizes economic relationships and builds economic models but business economics adopts, modifies and reformulates economic models to suit the specific conditions to solve the problems of the firm.
6. Economic theory makes some assumptions whereas business economics introduces certain feed backs.

Scope of Business Economics

Business economics is a solution oriented subject to the problems of the Business organisation, and the problems in whatever in its form. Since the business is dynamic and numerous problems are emerging in the day to day business, there is no uniformity in the scope of business economics among various authors. The following aspects (areas) are identified as the fields that come under the purview of business economics.

1. Demand Analysis and demand forecasting
2. Cost and production analysis
3. Pricing decisions, policies and practices
4. Profit management and
5. Capital management
6. In other areas:
   (*a*) Business economics and statistics
   (*b*) Business economics and mathematics
   (*c*) Business economics and accounting
   (*d*) Business economics and operations research
   (*e*) Business economics and the theory of decision-making

1. Demand analysis and demand forecasting. The business firms convert their economic resources in to a saleable products or services. These business units should know as to what are the factors that influence the demand for their goods or services? What would be the total demand for their existing product or new methods? How to forecast the demand for their products or services? What are the existing methods of forecasting their demand? All these questions call for proper business planning and occupy a vital or strategic place in Business Economics.

2. Cost and production analysis. The demand for the product depends upon the several factors, one among them is the cost of a product or service. There is a need to build up proper cost data of the organisation. The study of types of cost and their behaviour in different periods is essential for control of costs and decision-making purposes. The study of scale of production, economies and diseconomies of production and the functional relationship between Inputs and Outputs also come under the scope of business economics.

3. Pricing decisions, policies and practices. The pricing is a very important area of Business Economics. The opening of economies through liberalisation, privatisation and globalisation to the free market; the pricing of a product became strategic and even changed the accounting system. Pricing of a product, methods of pricing, pricing in different types of markets, factors to be considered in the pricing of a product are the important areas to be studied under business economics.

4. Profit management. The main objective of the business concern is to earn profit and also maximization of profits. Profit is the barometer to measure the performance of the business organisation. Hence the profit management constitutes the scope of business economics. This is possible through the better management of costs and selling price. The profit management covers profit measurements, profit policies and techniques of profit planning like Break Even Analysis.

5. Capital management. Capital Management is one of the crucial aspects of business economics. The success of a business organisation mainly depends upon the deployment of its capital on fixed assets, investments and current assets. It requires adequate knowledge and skill to manage the capital while deploying it on assets. The capital management implies planning and control of capital expenditure through better management of cost of capital, rate of return and selection of projects.

6. Other areas. In recent years, the development of mathematical and statistical techniques for analyzing situations faced by the business economists have prompted their use in the Decision-Making process. Hence the scope of business economics is widened to other areas, which are discussed here.

(*a*) **Business economics and statistics.** Statistics is widely used by the business economist. First it calls for the mastering in quantitative data and reaching useful measure of appropriate functional relationships involved in decision-making. Secondly, business economics employs statistical methods for empirical testing of economic generalizations. Finally, managers do not usually have exact information about the variables affecting decisions and have got to deal with the uncertainty of future events.

(*b*) **Business economics and mathematics.** Mathematics provides a set of tools, which help in the derivation, and exposition of economic analysis. Business economics is metrical because it estimating economic relationships and predict the relevant economic factors for decision-making and forward planning. While estimating and predicting the economic factors the mathematical tools and concepts such as Logarithms and Exponential, Vectors, Determinants and Matrix Algebra, Calculus, differential, integral are used.

(*c*) **Business economics and operations research.** The significant relationship between business economics and operations research can be highlighted with reference to certain important problem of managerial economics which are solved with the help of operations research techniques like linear programming, inventory models, game theory etc. The problems of business economics are allocation problems, competitive problems, waiting line problems and inventory problems.

(*d*) **Business economics and accounting.** Business economics is also related to accounting. Accounting is concerned with recording the financial operations of a business firm and also it is source of data for decision making. The profit and loss accounting will help the business economist to decide whether to continue with the same product or discontinue with the production. It helps to identify the variable, which should be controlled, increased or decreased and so on.

(*e*) **Business economics and the theory of decision-making.** The theory of decision-making is relatively a new subject that has significance in business economics. The economic theory is based on single goal *i.e.,* maximizing of profits. The theory of decision-making recognizes the multiplicity of goals and pervasiveness of uncertainty in the real world of management.

Business operations and business environment

In the process of management decision-making several factors influence the business. These factors can be classified in to internal factors or business operations since these factors are the business activities within the firm, which influence the business and external factors which are not in the purview of the internal activities of the business firm.

Business operations

There are certain factors which are controllable or within the control of business houses; such as cost, quality, reduction of wastage, increasing productivity, team development, increasing the skill, abilities and knowledge of workforce, and the like. They are within the bounds of business, hence, they are called as business operation. The decision-makers have to use their due diligence, acumen for the betterment of the businesses by developing these factors for better development of business activities.

In simple words ***Business operations are the internal factors that lie within the scope and operations of a firm and hence within the control of management.***

Business Environment

Business, it is said, is a product of environment. The nature of business, location of a business environment; the product to be manufactured or service to be rendered by the business unit; the price to be fixed and other related factors relating to the business unit are determined by the environment within which the business operates.

There are certain factors which are uncontrollable or beyond the control of business houses but which have considerable influence or bearing on the business such as political - legal, technological, economic, socio-cultural, globalization, and natural environmental factors.

The business environment poses threats to a firm or offers immense, opportunities for potential market exploitation.

William F. Glueck and **Lawrence R. Jauch** describes thus *"the environment include factors outside, the firm which can lead to opportunities for or threats to the firm. Although there are many factors, the most important of the sectors are socio- economic, technological, supplier, competitors and government".*[7]

In simple words ***the external factors lie outside the control of management because they are external to the firm and are said to constitute business environment.***

The Role of Business Economist

Business economists play a very important role in the business to achieve the predetermined goals of an organisation. The business is dynamic in nature hence the duty or task of business economist is also fast changing. The following are some of the chief or important tasks of a business economist.

Role of Business Economist

1. Identifying various business problems
2. Providing quantitative information
3. Acting as a thinker, friend and philosopher
4. Economic adviser to the firm
5. Quickly responding to the dynamic changes
6. Conduct various types of research studies
7. Synthesize the policies of different departments

1. **To identify various business problems.** The business is in dynamic society, and hence there is a fast changing business environment. The business economist has to identify the various business problems, their causes, consequences and also suggest remedial measures to resolve these problems.
2. **To provide a quantitative information.** The decisions of the business firm are taken on the basis of the previous year's quantitative information. The business economist has to create database for decision making and forward planning in the business organization. For example the production or sales of the firm for the next period is always based on the previous years' sales. The planning activities of the

[7] Glueck and Jauch, Business Policy and Strategic Management, p.95

business organisation are also on the basis of the previous year's information or facts and figures.

3. **To act as a thinker, friend and philosopher.** The business economist is involved in the day today business and with a wide knowledge of business and the external business world. He acts as a thinker and focusses on the impact of changing environment on business. He should act like a friend and come to the rescue of the business organisation whenever there is threat to the business. He should also suggest the organization with his forecasting vision.
4. **To act as economic adviser to the firm.** The business economist is well versed in the Economic aspects of the country like resource constraints, inflation, employment, trade cycles, balance of payments, global business threats etc. He must advise the firm about the impact of all these aspects of economy on the business decisions in the process of decision making.
5. **He should quickly respond to the dynamic changes.** The business economist should respond to dynamic changes in the business world on the decision-making policies of the business. For example the business economist must profess the impact of emergencies and sudden happenings like the gulf war, economic recession, import restrictions, dumping policies, globalisation, Asian crisis etc., on the business in pricing policy, production policy etc, well on time so that the company can act and earn reasonable profit.
6. **To conduct various types of research studies.** The business economist must conduct various types of research studies like customer's perception of the product and its impact on the sales, impact of monetary and fiscal policies on the performance of the company, impact of globalisation on the performance of the business and its strategies. Research studies must leads to solutions for the business problems and in turn help the management to take right decisions.
7. **To synthesize various policies formulated by different departments.** The success of the organisation depends on the integration of all the departments, the business economist must integrate the policies of various departments like production, purchasing, finance, marketing, R and D etc for the over all success of the firm. Hence all the departments are inter related because the production department produces goods only when departments like finance, purchasing, marketing, personnel departments co-operate by supplying required finance by the finance department, employees by the personnel dept. sales by the sales dept. and datasharing etc.,
8. **To have complete information about the environmental factors.** The business economist must have complete information about the business environment factors internal and external, which influence the business. The internal factors that influence the business are volume of output, wages and wage policy, pricing policy, credit policy etc. The external factors are business cycles, availability of raw materials, foreign policy of the country etc.,

Responsibilities of a Business Economist

In the process of achieving the predetermined tasks of the business organisation the business economist has to own some responsibilities and discharge certain duties. They are:

Responsibilities of Business Economist

1. Ensure profit to the organisation
2. Make successful business forecasts
3. Creat good trend to management
4. Maintain contact with individuals and data sources
5. Interpreting and explain the economic literature
6. Preparing business speeches to executives
7. Participate in public debates, workshop, seminars etc.,
8. Enhance his own status in the organisation.

1. **To ensure reasonable amount of profit to the organisation.** The success or failure of the organisation depends upon the profitability of the firm hence he should help the organisation in earning reasonable amount of profit. If the organisation earns reasonable amount of profit, it increases the reputation of the company, the value of the shares in the market etc.
2. **To make successful forecasts of the organisation.** Future is uncertain. The success of any business depends on the forecasts that the business organisation does. Hence the business economist must make short term and long term forecasts of the production, sales, distribution, profit, finance etc.
3. **To assure a particular trend to management.** With the rich experience and business knowledge the business economist should see that a particular good trend should be created in production, sales and profit to the management to declare dividend and to increase the wealth of the shareholders.
4. **To establish and maintain contact with individuals and data sources.** The success of the business depends on accuracy of forecast. The accuracy of forecast depends upon the sources of data and the contacts of the business economist with the awareness of available sources and personal contacts. He should join professional associations and take active interest in them.
5. **To interpret and explain economic literature to management.** The important responsibility of the business economist is to analyse the available data and interpret the data to the management in the form of value added statements, tables, charts and diagrams through power point presentation for effective communication.
6. **To prepare speeches for business executives.** Since the executives doesn't have the overall knowledge of the business and business environment, the business economist must prepare speeches to the business executives to present them in the workshops and seminars at national and international level to represent the organisation. Now a days the success of the company depends upon how the business executives present the information of the company to the customers at various exhibitions, seminars, workshops, discussion tables etc.
7. **To participate in public debates, work shops, seminars etc. to update the knowledge.** The business economist must participate in public debates, workshops and seminars and interact with the competent persons and update his knowledge. This in turn helps the management to take right decisions with the updated knowledge.
8. **To enhance his own status in the organisation.** The business economist must identify himself in the organisation through his knowledge, involvement in the successful running of the company.

Uses of Business Economics

The business manger has to take several decisions in his day to day business and also he has to do forward planning. For the successful decision-making and forward planning, the manager must have the thorough knowledge of business economics. The business economics is useful to the business manager in several ways. They are discussed below.

Uses of Business Economics
1. It provides suitable tool kit of economic principles to solve business problems
2. Incorporates useful ideas from other disciplines
3. Reaching a variety of business decisions
4. Makes a manager more competent model builder
5. Serves as an integrating agent
6. Acts as an agent between firm and society.

1. The business economics **provides a suitable tool kit from traditional economics** to solve the problem of business management. From the economics tool kit he can pick relevant economic principles or theory or economic concepts to solve the business problems.
2. It **incorporates useful ideas from other disciplines** like psychology, sociology, statistics etc., for decision making. The application of psychological theories to the business practice is necessary. For example the study of the Maslow's theory helps the marketing manager to study the movement of human beings from basic needs to safety needs, security needs and self-actualization needs. Based on this he can diversify the production.
3. It **helps in reaching a variety of business decisions** in a complicated environment like what to produce, techniques of production, inputs of productions prices, size and locations of new plants etc.
4. It **makes a manager a more competent model builder.** The business economics helps the manager to prepare some model to achieve objectives through his experience and research study.
5. It **serves as an integrating agent** in the functional areas like production dept, purchase dept, personel, finance, marketing department etc., of the business firm to achieve even conflicting goals.
6. It acts as an **agent between firm and society** and tries to accomplish the role of attaining economic and social welfare.

QUESTIONS ON THE CHAPTER

(Two marks)

1. Define Business Economics?
2. Is Business Economics a Positive science or Normative Science?
3. What is meant by Decision-Making ?
4. What does Forward Planning mean?

5. Is Business Economics a Microeconomics? Why?

6. What does Positive Science mean?

7. Is Business Economics is a Normative Science? Why?

8. Whether Business Economics is positive or normative. If so why?

9. What do you mean by Business Environment?

10. What do you mean by Business Operations?

11. Distinguish between Business Environment and Business Operations.

(Five marks)

1. Mention and discuss the chief characteristic features of Business Economics.

2. Explain the objectives of the Business Economics.

3. Distinguish between Business Economics and Economics.

4. Discuss the scope of Business Economics.

Essay Type Questions (Fifteen marks)

1. What is meant by Business Economics? Explain the role and responsibilities of Business Economist.

2. Define Business Economics. Discuss the significance of the study of Business Economics to a Business Manager.

3. Define Business economics? Explain its characteristics.

SKILL DEVELOPMENT

The skill development component is unique in the B.Com syllabus but not in Business Economics. It depends upon the teacher's inclination to the subject, interest, involvement and analytical bent of mind. The teacher can imbibe the skill development to the students by asking objective type questions or giving live small case studies, facilitating the students in the course of discussion and so on. In this book we made some efforts to develop some practices in this direction.

1. Make the students to prepare organisation chart of a manufacturing industry.

2. Decision making process

The Role of Business Economist is vital in the companies' decision making process. In each stage of business, commencing from the idea generation to the product is sold and even after sales, he helps the top management in the process of solving the problems of the business. Let us take an example that you have Rs. 10,00,000 in your hand and want to start a business project, then the role of business economist starts at the beginning of the production itself by self questioning and answering some of the questions of the various functional departments.

(*a*) *Production Department*

What product to produce / manufacture?

Who are the competitors?

What is the design of your product?

What are the product strengths in design?

What is the level of production quantity?

What is the demand forecast for your product?

(*b*) *Marketing Department*

How do you conduct market survey?

What are the pricing methods of competitors?

What is your method of pricing?

What is the product life cycle?

What are the pricing strategies of your competitors?

What is your pricing strategy?

What is the network of channel of distribution?

What are your methods of motivating distributors?

What is your promotional strategy?

What are your media of advertisement, its timings and so on?

How many days you advertising your product?

(*c*) *Finance Department*

What is the total capital / funds required for the project?

What is the extent of long term capital / funds, its sources and composition?

What is the extent of short-term capital / funds, its sources and composition?

How to raise the funds / capital?

What is break even point?

What are the risks involved in raising funds? Whether they are high risk or low risk?

Make or buy decisions?

Rate of return - capital employed?

(*d*) *General Decisions*

Where to incorporate the company?

What are the incentives / encouragement's offered by various state governments?

What is the policy of the state government towards encouraging the projects?

What are the resources or factors of production available in the state in which you decided to start your project?

Think about the stability of state government and central government and their policies.

3. With Rs. 500 you will go to a books shop to purchase the goods required for your semester. You will find books written by various authors in each subject. But you will select one book on each subject of the semester. This process of selection is called what?
4. Assume you are an entrepreneur and give one example of your forward planning in the process of Competition and diversification of products.

CHAPTER

2

CONSUMER BEHAVIOUR

CHAPTER OUTLINE	LEARNING OBJECTIVES
What is consumer ? — Difference between a consumer and customer — What is consumer behavior? — Consumer sovereignty Meaning of consumer sovereignty — Manifestations of consumer sovereignty — Limitations of consumer sovereignty — Is consumer sovereignty desirable? — Approaches to the study of consumer behaviour — Cordinal or marshallian approach — The law of equi-marginal utility — The law of consumer surplus — Ordinal approach — The indifference curve analysis	After studying this chapter, you should be able to : 1. Define who is consumer? 2. Differentiate between a consumer and a customer 3. Know what consumer behavior is 4. Know what is consumer sovereignty 5. Decide whether consumer sovereignty is desirable 6. Understand cordinal and ordinal utility approach 7. Understand the meaning, assumptions, importance, criticisms of law of equi-marginal utility 8. Define what is indifference curve 9. Know what is IC schedule and scale of preference 10. What are the properties of IC 11. Know the superiority of IC over marshallian approach 12. Know what MRS is? 13. Understand all about consumer surplus

An organisation has to think from the point of view of the consumer and also from the point of the person who purchases the goods or services for others called customer. For example when a toy is purchased for a child, the manager of the organisation must bother about the parents' behaviour towards the toy. In characterizing consumer behaviour, there are two important but distinct factors to consider: consumer opportunities and consumer preferences.[8] Consumer opportunities are the possible goods and services offered by the producer for the consumer's consumption. Consumers' preferences are the goods which are preferred for the consumption according to his fashions, tastes and so.

Out of the goods and services offered by the producer, consumer may or may not have the goods to consume. For example there are many electrical products offered by the Philips in the market. But consumers select only some of them according to their tastes and preferences. Similarly Reliance Info-com offered several schemes of mobile phone services, but market i.e., customers accepted only a few schemes. In today's market there is a need to study the behaviour of the consumer towards the products offered, prices, quality, product preferences, product features, accessibility to the customer, methods of accessibility, media to be selected to inform and appeal a customer. All these initiate to make a study of the consumer behavior. Hence the study must focus on the position of consumer in the market, factors of demand and its analysis, utility of a commodity and the pattern of behavior.

Now let us discuss who is a consumer and what is the difference between a consumer and customer. Consumer is one who actually consumes the product and becomes the end user of the product. Consumer is different from the customer. The customer is one who purchases the goods for the sake of others consumption for examples if a father purchases a motor cycle to a son through a dealer, then the father and dealer are the customers and the son is a consumer. Here the manufacturer of the motor cycle should manufacture the motor cycle as per the needs and requirements of the consumer in design, color, quality, fuel consumption, price and the like. Hence the manufacturer of the motor cycles continuous to modify the motor bikes as per the needs of consumers and also to compete with the competitors in the market, hence he conducts market research and updates the changes throughout the product life cycle. Then only he can remain in the market and make gains.

CONSUMERS' SOVEREIGNTY

In a free enterprise market oriented economy, the role played by the consumers is a central one, because his choices determine as to which goods should be produced and in what quantities, color, shape, design etc. Every producer without knowing consumer's taste and preferences cannot start production. In India, there are large numbers of product failures in as much as the producers this is due to not making any attempt to collect and analyse the data to understand the customer's tastes and preferences. They went on manufacturing the goods and rendering services blindly and mechanically, as a result they have suffered heavy losses and burnt their fingers, the living example is Le-sancy soap, All India Radio, Fiat car, cigarettes for women and the like.

Under capitalism, the consumer is the "King". The argument in which this proposition is based as follows: ***the immediate purpose of all productive activity in a capitalistic economy is to sell goods to the consumer.*** The money income of the producer comes from the price paid by the consumer, hence producers try to bring such goods to the market as would give

---

[8] Michael R. Baye, "Managerial Economics and Business Strategy" McGraw-Hill Higher Education, international edition, p.113.

satisfaction to the consumer. It is the consumer's preference, which ultimately decides what is to be produced, therefore consumer is the "King", Sovereign, and Monarch.

The ultimate objective of our modern business is consumer satisfaction. Although the concept of consumer satisfaction is new to us, it is not new to the westerners, because of their literacy level, awareness, ability to exercise as a right and their ability to pay and so on. In India the consciousness of consumer satisfaction is improving because of the acceptance of LPG (Liberalisation, Privatisation and Globalisation) under the new economic policy. With these economic reforms in India, the platforms like consumers' forum, consumer courts, consumers' grievances redress cells, consumer movements are in infant stage.

MEANING OF CONSUMER SOVEREIGNTY

Consumer sovereignty is an important concept in explaining the role of consumption in a market economy. The concept of consumer's sovereignty is appropriate in a capitalistic economy. The producer in a market economy produces goods according to the requirements of the consumer. ***Consumer is the central focus of any productive activity. The needs of consumer will convert in to want, if the want is backed by ability to pay will become demand for that commodity. The demands of consumers will come in the form of a product.*** Hence he is the central point in the market and marketing activities of the economy. Consumer sovereignty means the consumer's freedom to select the product of their choice.

Consumer sovereignty can be defined as *"the significant role which consumer plays in determining the productive effort of the country."*

Prof. Benham points out that "Under capitalism consumer is the King". He prepares his expenditure plan on the basis of his own likes and dislikes.

In simple words, the supremacy of the consumer in selecting and consuming any type of goods and services on the basis of his own tastes and preferences is popularly known as consumers' sovereignty. It is also called as 'freedom of choice'.

MANIFESTATION OF CONSUMERS' SOVEREIGNTY

In a capitalistic economy the consumers' sovereignty is manifested in the following manner.

Manifestation
1. All productive activities of the producer
2. Freedom and to channel the resources
3. Determination of market price
4. Distribution of income among the agents
5. Operation of market mechanism
6. Volume of economic welfare

1. **All productive activities of the producer depend on consumer's decisions.** In a capitalistic economy the producer produces his products based on the consumer's tastes, preferences, fashions, color, design, price, additional features in the product etc.
2. **Freedom of resource owners (raw materials, land, capital etc.,) to channel their resources depends upon consumers' decision.** The resources of the owners

are designed or directed with the intentions of satisfying the consumers' needs. For example the intentions of supplying raw material is to provide quality product to consumer or supplying capital or organisation skill is to serve the consumer with a quality product at reasonable price.

3. **Determination of market price depends on consumers' decision.** The market prices of a commodity or service produced, is determined with the intention of satisfying the needs of the consumers. For example, in India because of liberalisation the MNCs started to compete with the Indian companies through the quality but the Indian companies challenged the MNCs in the price, hence the Indian companies sustained in the market and the MNCs later realized the market reality and reduced their market price. For example in the case of electronic goods like TVs, DVDs, refrigerators.
4. **Distribution of income among the agents of production depends on consumers' decision.** The income distribution among the agents of production like men, material, machine, money etc., is with the intention of providing product or service is to serve the consumer with good product at competitive prices and so on.
5. **Operation of market mechanism depends on consumers' decisions.** The operation of market mechanism like supply and demand to determine the price of a product and to provide adequate product depends upon consumer decisions.
6. **Volume of economic welfare depends upon consumers' decisions.** The welfare activities in an organisation determine the extent of consumers concern in that economy.

FACTORS LIMITING CONSUMERS' SOVEREIGNTY

In real and actual life, the so-called consumer's sovereignty is limited or restricted by the following factors.

Factors Limiting Consumers' Sovereignty

1. Size of money income
2. Productive capacity of the economy
3. Level of technology
4. Restrictions of the government
5. Tax structure
6. Monopoly and imperfect competition
7. Fashion and customs
8. Inflation
9. Advertisement
10. The level of income
11. During wartime

1. **Size of money income.** Production is governed by effective demand and this in turn depends on the income of the consumer. When the income is very much limited, the freedom of choice is restricted. If a majority of consumers sovereignty become a myth. Strictly in a capitalistic economy, the rich people (who are in a minority) have greater-influence in deciding what is to be produced than the poor who constitutes the majority

of the consumers example Rolls Royce, Corolla, Mercedes Benz Cars, Johnson's baby toilet soap, droppers, Tanishq Jewellary and the like.

2. **Productive capacity of the economy.** The standard of people is determined by the productive capacity of the economy. For example in USA the standard of living of the people is more, hence they have ample opportunities to select any of the products produced in any country. In this economy consumers' sovereignty prevails because of their standard of living and productive capacity. Where as in developing countries the consumer's choice is restricted due to limited purchasing powers and also for want of raw materials or of hi-tech machinery also.
3. **Level of technology.** The level of technology in the economy influences the consumers by providing alternatives to select the superior products. For example because of globalisation many of the consumers in India are fortunate to have highly superior products of their choice like TV sets, Motor cars, Computers, electronic goods etc.
4. **Restrictions of the government.** The Government controls consumption of some goods through rationing or priorities or control over production. If government imposes restrictions on the goods through rationing, control over the fashions, preferences of the consumers, then there will be less consumer sovereignty.
5. **Tax structure.** The existing tax structure of the country may also affect the consumer's choice. The heavy excise duty and income tax imposed by the government increases the price of commodities and reduces the purchasing power of consumer. Hence in both the cases consumers choice is restricted.
6. **Monopoly and imperfect competition.** Consumer enjoys full freedom and dictates production only in perfectly competitive market conditions. But in practice, markets are not perfect and free. For instance in many industries, monopoly and monopolistic competitions will curtail the liberty of the consumer.
7. **Fashion and customs.** The customs and fashions prevalent in that country adversely affects the freedom of choice of the consumer. For example in Islamic countries their custom and fashion influence the women fashionable products and dresses like jeans pant. Acceptance of fashions and customs will determine the consumers' sovereignty. If there is restriction on fashion because of customs, the consumer sovereignty will reduce and vice versa.
8. **Inflation.** Inflation in an economy will influence the purchasing power of the people. Consumers cannot purchase as per their wishes so it restricts their sovereignty.
9. **Advertisement.** Advertisement and publicity through mass media like FM Radio, Television, Newspapers, Magazines etc., will exercise powerful influence on the consumers' tastes and preferences. In modern days, sellers can influence consumer's choice through advertisement and clever salesmanship with the intention of earning more profit. For example in India the brand ambassadors of the product Pepsi are Mr. Shahruk Khan and Sachin Tendulkar who are influencing the consumer's demand.
10. **The level of income.** The consumers are also producers. Their income depends on the volume of investment and employment in the society. Variations in the amount of investment and employment cause changes in the income of the consumer and affect his scale of preference.
11. **During wartime.** The consumer's sovereignty is seriously reduced under rationing during the times of war. In capitalistic countries, rationing of commodities is introduced

and all essential commodities are restricted in such a way as to get equality between supply and demand.

Is Consumer's Sovereignty Desirable?

According to classical and neo-classical economists, consumer's sovereignty is desirable or beneficial to the society because this would help consumers in getting maximum satisfaction. But the socialists vehemently oppose the freedom of choice granted to the consumers on the following grounds:

1. In the first place, they pointed out that monopolistic capitalists ***exploit the consumer*** and instead of being a sovereign, he is reduced to the position of slave.
2. In the second place, the freedom of consumer's choice led to ***wrong and un-economic utilization of resources.***
3. In the third place, the socialists attacked on the ground that by allowing full freedom of choice, ***the consumer's are likely to injure themselves.***

We can conclude that the consumer's choice is not absolute, he is neither a sovereign nor a slave.

APPROACHES TO THE STUDY OF CONSUMER BEHAVIOUR

The study of consumer behaviour is more relevant to a producer or to a Manager of a company. The study of consumer behavior has the following approaches.

There are four approaches in the study of consumer behaviour. They are:

1. The Marginal Utility approach or Marshallian approach or Cardinal approach
2. Indifference Curve (Technique) approach or analysis, or Ordinal approach.
3. Samuelsons' Revealed Preference Theory and
4. Hicks' Logical Weak Ordering Theory.

The Marginal Utility approach or Cardinal approach. Cardinal approach is an approach which assumes that utility of a commodity is measurable in terms of numerical units. For example, according to this approach the consumer can measure the utility from an apple as 20 units from orange as 10 units.

The laws, which are studied under this approach, are:

1. The Law of Diminishing Marginal Utility
2. The Law of Equi-Marginal Utility
3. The Theory of Demand
4. The Law of Consumer Surplus

Ordinal approach: Ordinal approach is an approach in which utility cannot be measured but it can be arranged in order and ranking is possible on the basis of preference. For example the utility derived from an orange is 10 units and from an apple is 20 units, which is double of an orange like this we can compare or we can arrange them in ranks. The Law, which is studied under this approach:

1. The Indifference Curve Analysis

DISTINCTION BETWEEN CARDINAL AND ORDINAL APPROACH

The following are the differences between Cardinal and Ordinal approach.

1. Cardinal approach is called classical approach in which utility or satisfaction has been made measurable. Whereas the ordinal approach in which utility can not be measured but it says that on the basis of consumers preferences, the commodities are ordered or ranked as first, second, third etc.
2. The cardinal numbers 1,2,3,4 etc., are used to quantify the utilities like an orange may yield 20 units of utility, whereas an apple yields an utility of 30 units. From this it is clear that the utility derived from apple is one and half times more than an orange. It is an imaginary one. Whereas the ordinal approach uses measurements like 1st, 2nd, 3rd etc. it helps to know the actual size of the related numbers. Here the 2nd need not be twice as that of the first.
3. Cordinal approach is a mental concept, cannot be measured and the quantified is not rational. Whereas the ordinal approach measure the utility on the basis of consumers preference like consumer prefers apple to an orange and rank the commodities in the scale of preference without taking trouble.
4. Dr. Marshall and his followers advocated the cardinal approach to utility. Whereas modern economists like prof. Hicks and Allen supported the ordinal approach

THE MARGINAL UTILITY APPROACH OR CARDINAL APPROACH

The student must know the following concepts before studying the utility theories.

Utility: Utility is construed as *"The want satisfying capacity or power of a commodity or service in the process of consumption"*. It means that the consumer gets utility to the extent to which the commodity satisfies his want. For example the utility of water is more when we are thirsty, hence we are ready to pay more than fourteen rupees for a litre of mineral water. The utility of piece of chalk to a teacher is more hence he will be ready to pay a little bit more than the normal price, whereas to a mason its utility is nil hence he would not be ready to pay anything for it.

To understand the utility clearly there is a need to understand the differences between Utility and Satisfaction.

Differences between Utility and Satisfaction

1. Utility is an expected satisfaction, whereas satisfaction is a realised satisfaction. This realised satisfaction is obtained after consumption.
2. The consumption of a product or service is required to get satisfaction, whereas for utility, actual consumption is not required.
3. Utility can be measured, though indirectly, whereas satisfaction cannot be measured directly or indirectly.

Total Utility: Total utility is the amount of utility derived from the consumption of all the units at the disposal of a consumer. According to A L Mayers, *"Total utility is the sum of marginal utilities associated with the consumption of successive units."* For example if a consumer consumes five units of a commodity then the total utility is the aggregate or sum of utilities derived from the consumption of all these five units. For example (20 + 18 + 15 + 10 + 4) = 67 units (see Table 2.1).

Table 2.1

The table showing the utility and total utility from the consumption of a commodity 'X'

Units of Commodity 'X'	*Utility (units of satisfaction)*	*Total utility (units of satisfaction)*
1	20	20
2	18	38
3	15	53
4	10	63
5	4	67

Marginal Utility: Marginal utility is the utility derived from an additional unit or Marginal utility is the addition made to the total utility with the consumption of an additional unit. For example, in the table 2.2 the total utility from the consumption of the fourth unit is 63 units, with the consumption of the fifth unit the total utility increased to 67 then the addition made to the total utility from the consumption of fifth unit is 4 units. These 4 units of utility is called marginal utility from an additional fifth unit.

Table 2.2

The table showing marginal utility

Units of consumption of commodity 'X'	*Total utility (units of satisfaction)*	*Marginal utility (units of satisfaction)*
1	20	20
2	38	18
3	53	15
4	63	10
5	67	4

THE LAW OF EQUI-MARGINAL UTILITY

The main intention of consumer or an entrepreneur is to earn maximum satisfaction and profits respectively within the available (limited) means. Sometimes the consumer may come to a situation wherein he has to purchase two or more goods within the available money or capital resource, if it is scarce, and intends to get maximum satisfaction. Similarly the producer or an entrepreneur has to decide which alternative factors of production, he has to select? What are the combinations of alternative factors of production? And what quantities of these factors will give maximum profits out of his limited money? Answers to all these questions are taken care by the principles of economics. One of these is the law of equi-marginal utility.

The law of equi-marginal utility is an extension of law of diminishing marginal utility. The law of D.M.U explains the equilibrium of consumers, consuming only one commodity, whereas in the real life we consume more than two commodities. Such a real life situation is explained under the principle of Law of Equi-Marginal Utility. This law explains the consumers' equilibrium when many commodities are consumed.

The law of equi-marginal utility is also known as the **Law of Maximum Satisfaction.** According to this law every consumer tries to get maximum satisfaction by using his limited income. It is also known as **Law of Substitution**, because the consumer goes on substituting the commodity whose marginal utility is more with a commodity that has less marginal utility till maximum satisfaction is attained. This law is called as the **Law of Equi-marginal Returns** as the entrepreneur, in the case of production will be spending on different factors of production is such a way that at the point of margin, returns are the same.

The Law of Equi-Marginal Utility is based on the three characteristics of wants viz., comparative, substitutable and complementary wants.

STATEMENT OF THE LAW

The law states that "Other things being equal, a consumer gets maximum total utility from spending his given income, when he allocates his expenditure to the purchase of different goods in such a way that the marginal utilities derived from the last unit of money spent on each item of expenditure tends to be equal". It is worth to mention the contention of Donald Waston. In his book **'Price Theory and its Uses'** he contends that when a consumer has some quantity of a commodity, he allocates the units among the several uses of the commodity in such a way as to get maximum satisfaction. In our daily life we face the situations when we have scare resources. For example you have a gold of 100 grams from that you have to get manufacture jewelry like necklace, bangles, chain, brace light, etc. Then you finally decide to allocate the gold on various jewelries in such a way that the utility of the last unit (gram) of gold spent tends to be equal.

Definitions

The definition is based on several assumptions. One important assumption is called *'Ceteris Paribus'*. It is a Latin term, which means 'other things remain constant or same for analysis. For *e.g.* in the above definition the prices of goods, money income and marginal utility of money will remain same or constant and other factors will change.

*The law has been stated by **Marshall** in these words: "If a person has a thing which can be put to several uses, he will distribute it among these uses in such a way that it has the same marginal utility, for if it had a greater marginal utility in one use than in another, he would gain by taking away some of it from the second use and applying it to the first."*

***William Fellner** states that "the rational consumer will distribute his purchase between the two goods in such a way that the marginal utility of the expenditure he makes for commodity 'A' should equal the marginal utility of the expenditure he makes for commodity 'B'.*

*According to **Boulding,** "The best division of expenditure is that at which the weighted marginal utilities in all lines of expenditure are equal".*

*According to **Samuelson** "A consumer gets maximum satisfaction when the ratio of marginal utilities of all commodities that the utility of the last rupee spent on each is equal."*

Assumptions of Law

This law is based on the following assumptions.

Assumptions
1. Rational consumer
2. Cardinal approach
3. Perfect knowledge of utilities
4. Prices of the goods remains constant
5. Income of the consumer remains constant
6. MU of money remains constant
7. Wants and goods are substitutable

1. **Rational consumer.** This law assumes that the consumer is a rational being and aims at getting maximum satisfaction out of his available money income.
2. **Cardinal approach.** This law, since it is a Cardinal approach assumes that the utility of a commodity under consumption can be measured numerically.
3. **Perfect knowledge of utilities.** The consumer has a given scale of preferences of the goods in consideration to purchase for consumption and he has perfect knowledge of utilities to be derived.
4. **Prices of the goods.** The Law of Equi-Marginal Utility assumes that the prices of the goods or services under consumption remain constant.
5. **Income of the consumer.** This Law assumes that the income of the consumer is constant, since it is a limiting factor to a consumer or a producer out of this limited income he must derive maximum satisfaction.
6. **Marginal utility of money.** The marginal utility of money should remain constant. The marginal utility of money is the increase in total utility of money resulting from the consumption of the marginal unit of money. For example the rich tend to spend money lavishly on goods or services, because of huge money they earn and show less importance to the utility derived from the money spent. In Indian economy we are observing that the urban population is showing less utility from the coins with denominations less than one rupee under circulation when compared to their counterparts (Rural). This is because every increment in money is tending to bring less and less pleasure in urban areas probably because of the high standard of living. This is due to the law of diminishing marginal utility. But in the law of Equi-Marginal Utility the Marginal Utility of money remains constant.
7. **Wants and goods are substitutable.** The law assumes that to satisfy wants, one good can be used in place of another. For example, to satisfy his thirsty a consumer he may buy water or cool drinks since most of the times the water and cool drinks are substitutable in place of one another.

Explanation of the Law

The principle of Equi-marginal utility can be explained with the help of an example. Let us assume that the money income of a consumer is Rs. 50 and he wants to purchase two commodities X and Y. The marginal utilities that he is deriving from the spending on both the goods are shown in the Table 2.3.

Table 2.3

The schedule showing the law of equi-marginal utility

Units of money expenditure (in Rs.)	*Marginal utility of expenditure on Commodity 'X' (in units)*	*Marginal utility of expenditure on Commodity 'Y' (in units)*
10	15	14
20	14	13
30	13	12
40	12	11
50	11	10
Total	65	60

Here the consumer has three alternatives.

(*a*) He can spend the entire income of Rs. 50 on 'X' commodity or

(*b*) He can spend the entire amount on 'Y' commodity or

(*c*) He can spend Rs. 50 on the combination of both the commodities.

If he spends his entire amount on commodity 'X' alone, he gets total marginal utilities of 65 units. If he spends his entire amount on Commodity 'Y' alone, he gets total marginal utility of 60 units. If he spends on the combination of both the commodities in such a way that the marginal utility of last unit of money spent tends to be equal (13 units of MU in each commodity) he gets total marginal utility of 69 units *i.e.,* **42** (15 + 14 + 13) and **27** (14 + 13). With highest marginal utility units he gets maximum satisfaction. (Price = MUs). In other words, consumer distributes his limited income in such a way so as to equate the marginal utility of expenditure on both the uses.

Diagrammatic Representation

This schedule can be represented diagrammatically by Fig. 2.1. In the diagram units of expenditure on X and Y commodity are shown on the left and right of the X-axis respectively. On OY axis the marginal utility of expenditure of both the commodities 'X' and 'Y' are represented. If the marginal utility of expenditure on commodity 'X' is plotted on a diagram marginal utility curve is obtained (MU 'X'). Similarly if the marginal utility of expenditure on commodity 'Y' is plotted on a diagram marginal utility curve is obtained called (MU 'Y'). The consumer spends Rs. 30 on commodity 'X' and Rs. 20 on commodity 'Y', which provides him the marginal utility of A and B. These two points are at an equal distance from the X-axis. This combination yields him maximum satisfaction. Any other combination will offer him less satisfaction for *e.g.,* if he spends Rs. 20 on commodity X and Rs. 30 on commodity Y, the loss in utility is more than the gain in utility. This is shown in the diagram by shaded area.

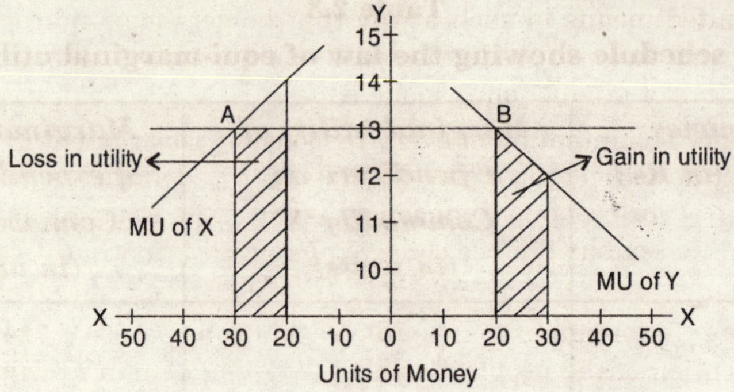

Fig. 2.1. The Law of Equi-Marginal Utility

William Fellner in his book 'Modern Economic Analysis' explains the rational consumers choice of this type with the help of Marginal Utility Expenditure (MUE) functions. He contends that the MUE for any goods is obtained by dividing the price of the good into marginal utility of the good itself, *i.e.,* the marginal utility of the good divided by its price. When the MUE on all the goods is same, the following relationship holds good:

$$\frac{\text{Marginal Utility of commodity X}}{\text{Price of commodity X}} = \frac{\text{Marginal Utility of commodity Y}}{\text{Price of commodity Y}}$$

That is to say,

$$\frac{\text{Marginal Utility of commodity X}}{\text{Marginal Utility of commodity Y}} = \frac{\text{Price of commodity X}}{\text{Price of commodity Y}}$$

These equations contain a summary of the marginal utility theory as a theory of rational consumer choice. In the words of Jack Hirshleifer, "For any commodity, MU divided by price is MU per dollar spent on that commodity. For the consumer not want to change his purchase rate of X relative to Y, the MU per dollar of X on Y, must be equal. The last dollar must yield equivalent satisfaction, whether spent on X or Y".

Significance or Usefulness of the law

This law is useful to the following users.

Usefulness of the law

1. To the consumer
2. To the producer
3. Government
4. In exchange
5. In price determination
6. In distribution

1. **To the consumer.** This law is useful to every consumer who aims at getting maximum satisfaction from his limited income. In order to achieve his goal of maximum satisfaction, he will go on substituting a commodity which gives more utility for a commodity which gives him lesser utility until the marginal utilities of the consumption of both the commodities are equal.

2. To the producer. The intelligent producer tries to employ the factors of production from his limited means in such a way that he gets maximum profit. He will go on substituting one factor of production with another factor, till marginal productivity of both the factors of production is made equal.

3. Government. The intention of every responsible government is to spend its limited public revenue collected or the funds borrowed from various sources for the development of an economy judiciously. This Law is useful to the government to spend its limited public finance collected in such a way that it gets maximum social benefits.

4. In exchange. In foreign exchange, the exchange is based on the law of substitution and the intention of the people also is to derive maximum earnings out of the goods they import and export. People exchange their goods and services in such a way that they get maximum satisfaction by replacing the goods which give more utility to the goods which yield less utility.

5. In price determination. This law is useful in the case of determining the price or value. The law of substitution comes to the rescue when there is scarcity of a commodity. This law gives knowledge to substitute the less scarce goods for the more scarce goods. The scarcity of the more scarce is thus relieved, and its price comes down. Price stability is maintained by transferring the goods from the place of plenty to scarcity.

6. In distribution. This law will help the employer to determine the rewards for the various factors of production like land, labour, capital and organisation. The rewards for such agents of production are rent, wages, interest and profit respectively. These rewards are determined according to the principle of marginal productivity. The process of distribution will go on till the marginal productivity of the factors is equal to their remuneration and the marginal productivity of different factors becomes.

Limitations or Exceptions of the Law

This law of Equi-marginal Utility suffers from the following limitations.

Exceptions of the Law

1. Indivisible goods
2. Budget period is indefinite
3. Resources are unlimited
4. Consumer's ignorance
5. Incompetent organizer
6. Big expenditure
7. Rational purchaser
8. Questionable assumptions

1. Indivisible goods. The law cannot be applied to indivisible goods, because when goods are indivisible, and the money available is limited, it becomes difficult to equate the marginal utilities. For *e.g.*, goods like house, a car, a TV set etc., are not easily divisible and if the money available is limited then one cannot buy both the commodities.

2. **Budget period.** The law cannot be applied to, if the budget period of a consumer is indefinite. But the law of Equi-marginal utility assumes that we have a definite quantity of resources within a given period, say a year or a month or a week.
3. **Resources are unlimited.** When resources are unlimited this law does not operate because, there would not be any problem to get maximum satisfaction out of unlimited resources. But in reality there are limited resources and unlimited wants.
4. **Consumer's ignorance.** This law does not operate when the consumer is ignorant of utility and cannot substitute the good which gives more utility to a good which gives less utility.
5. **Incompetent organizer.** The principle of Equi-marginal utility is also inapplicable in case of incompetent organizer as he does not know how to substitute one factor of production in place of another factor till the marginal utilities derived from both the factors are equal to earn maximum profits.
6. **Big expenditure.** An intelligent person applies the law with high thinking only if the expenditure on which money deployment is high and avails this law. If the expenditure is less he neglects the law.
7. **Rational purchaser.** This law is applied judiciously by rational purchaser in the case of purchases.
8. **Assumptions.** This law is based on some questionable assumptions like utility can be measured, comparable and the marginal utility of money remains constant in the successive purchases. The modern economists criticise the basic assumptions of this law.

INDIFFERENCE CURVE ANALYSIS

The indifference analysis is an alternative approach to the theory of consumer demand. This theory was developed because of the limitations of the cardinal approach or utility approach. This is an ordinal approach which states that utility cannot be measured but it can be arranged in order. Ranking is possible on the basis of preference. **Edgeworth** originated this technique of indifference curves in 1881 and an Italian Economist **Pareto** refined it in 1906. This technique, however, attained perfection and systematic application by **J. R. Hicks and R. G. D. Allen.** Hicks published a book "*Value and Capital*" in 1939 which throws light on his research studies.

The understanding of this theory calls for the understanding of some of the concepts. These concepts are discussed below.

Scale of preference. In this process of preference, the consumer or the enterprise makes mental calculation of the combination of goods before the purchase within the limited funds. If series of combinations from highest to the lowest level of satisfaction ranking is arrived at which is called the scale of preference. For example if the consumer has Rs. 50 but has to purchase apples and oranges, the consumer prepares the combinations mentally and ranks the order of these combinations on the basis of level of satisfaction.

Definition. *"The conceptual or mental arrangement of combination of two goods and services set in the order of the level of significance is called the scale of preference".*

This can be understood with the help of a Table 2.4.

Table 2.4
Scale of preference

Combination of commodity X and Y	*Level of satisfaction*	*Ranking the order of preference*
A. 12X + 12Y	Highest	I
B. 10X + 10Y	Lesser than combination A	II
C. 8X + 8Y	Lesser than combination A & B	III

Indifference schedule. If the consumer goes on making the combinations of goods and services that he wants to buy, then he will reach a stage where he prepares the list of combinations of these goods or services which gives him same level of satisfaction. Then the consumer can purchase any combination of these goods or services so that he gets same level of satisfaction.

Definition. *"it is a list of alternative combinations in the stocks of two goods which yield the same level of satisfaction to the consumer".*

The following table shows the indifference schedule.

Table 2.5
Indifference schedule

Combination	*Apple*	*Orange*	*Level of satisfaction*
A	1	12	Same
B	2	8	Same
C	3	5	Same
D	4	3	Same
E	5	2	Same

All the above combinations of two goods give same level of satisfaction.

Indifference curve. A curve that defines the combinations of two or more goods that give a consumer the same level of satisfaction is called indifference curve. This curve we get if we plot the above table on a graph.

Definition. *"It is the locus (center) of points representing all the different combination of two goods which gives equal level of satisfaction to the consumer".*

In the words of William Fellner, "An indifference curve shows for two commodities those combinations of commodity quantities which bring a consumer the same amount of satisfaction ('Utility')[9].

This can represented on the diagram as follows (Fig. 2.2)

[9] William Fellner, "Modern Economic Analysis, p. 181.

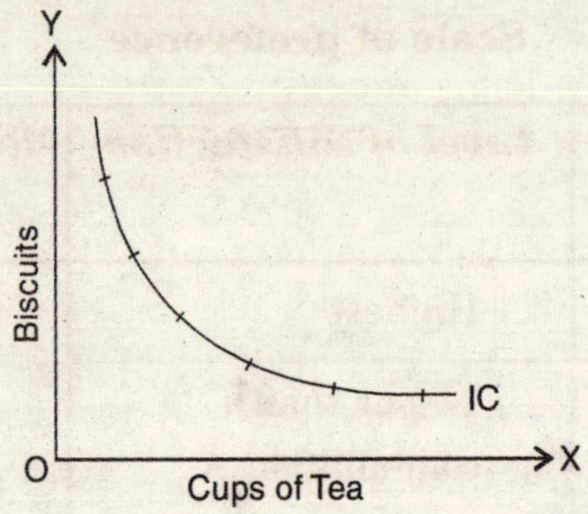

Fig. 2.2

On OX axis cups of tea is represented. On OY axis biscuits are represented. The various combinations of two goods, which give same level of satisfaction, are represented on a graph in the form of points. If you join all the points of various combinations of two goods, we get a curve called Indifference curve (IC). On this curve the consumer is indifferent to select any one of the combination because he gets same level of satisfaction from any combination.

Indifference map. The consumer can prepare any combination of two goods which gives him same level of satisfaction if the same is plotted on a graph we can get an Indifference curve. Similarly if he prepare list of combinations for the different amount (Budget) available then he will get different Indifference curves. If these indifference curves obtained from different amount (budget) are plotted on a graph, we get an Indifferent Map. On this Indifference Map each Indifference curve shown represents different level of satisfaction to a consumer because it is plotted from different amounts (budget). The Indifference curve, which is at higher point on the map, shows highest level of satisfaction and the Indifference curve at the lower point on the map shows lower level of satisfaction.

Definition. *"It is a set of indifference curves, each indifference curve represents different level of satisfaction. Higher the indifference curve represents higher level of satisfaction".*

The diagrammatic representation of Indifference Map is shown in figure 2.3

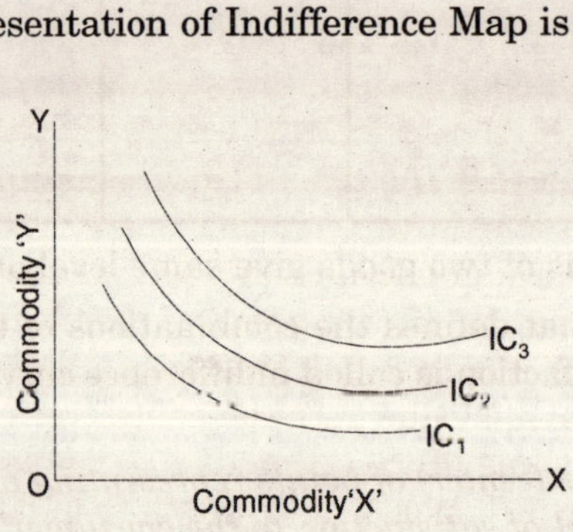

Fig. 2.3

Marginal rate of substitution (MRS): The shape of the indifference curve depends on the consumers' preferences. Different consumers generally will have indifference curves of different shapes. One important way to summarize information about a consumer is in terms of marginal rate of substitution.

Meaning of MRS: The rate at which a consumer is willing to substitute one good for another good and still maintain the same level of satisfaction is called MRS.

In **Hicks'** words, "we may define **marginal rate of substitution of X for Y as the quantity of Y which would just compensate the consumer for the loss of the marginal unit of X.**"[10]

The marginal rate of substitution will determine the shape of the Indifference curve. If the Diminishing marginal rate of substitution is there then the Indifference curve slopes downwards from left to right. If the marginal rate of substitution is in increasing trend, then the Indifference curves slopes upward from left to right. But according to the law of Indifference Curve the shape of MRS always slopes downwards, it is one of the properties of the law and it is always convex to the origin.

Diminishing marginal rate of substitution. *The rate at which one commodity is substituted for the consumption of another to maintain the same level of satisfaction is called diminishing marginal rate of substitution*. This phenomenon is due to the law of diminishing marginal utility which states that more the consumption, lesser would be the marginal utility.

Let us understand this diminishing marginal rate of substitution with the help of a Table 2.6

Table 2.6

Diminishing MRS of the commodities

Combination	*Commodity X*	*Commodity Y*	*MRS of commodity X and Y*
1	20	1	—
2	16	2	4 : 1
3	13	3	3 : 1
4	11	4	2 : 1
5	10	5	1 : 1

According to the Table 2.6, to acquire (Substitute) one unit of commodity Y, the consumer foregoes 4 units of commodity X. Here the MRS is 4:1. Similarly to acquire one more unit of commodity Y at the combination of 3, the consumer foregoes 3 units of commodity X, here the marginal rate of substitution is 3:1. At the combination of 4, the consumer foregoes 4 units of commodity X to acquire one extra unit of commodity Y, here the marginal rate of substitution is 2:1 and so on in the next combination. He foregoes one commodity for another to keep the same level of satisfaction. The MRS in the first unit was 4:1, in the subsequent units it was 3:1, 2:1 and 1:1. This rate goes on diminishing due to the law of Decreasing Marginal Utility. Hence this law is called the Law of Diminishing MRS. If the same is represented on a graph or diagram we will get an Indifference curve which slopes downwards from left to right.

On OX axis commodity Y is represented. On OY axis commodity X is represented. If we plot the above table we get an Indifference curve which slopes downwards from left to right. In the diagram the marginal rate of substitution AB is greater than CD and CD is greater than EF is greater than GH which is AB > CD > EF > GH and so on. See Fig. 2.4

[10] K K Dewett, "Modern Economic Theory", S. Chand & Company, New Delhi, p.53

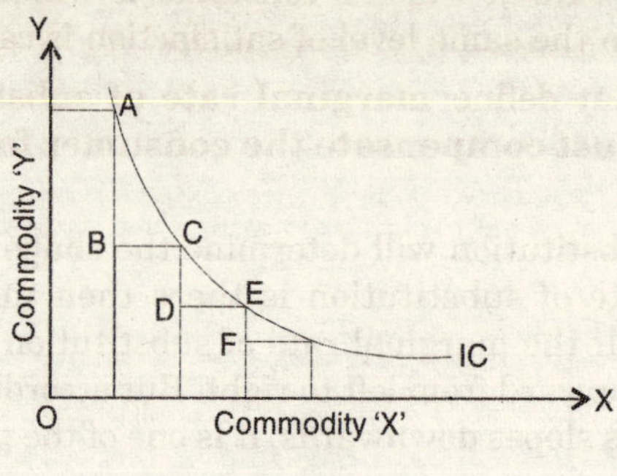

Fig. 2.4

Assumptions of Indifference Curve Technique or Analysis

This approach is based on the following assumptions.

1. Consumer is interested to buy two goods in combinations.
2. The consumer has to prepare his scale of preference.
3. The consumer always prefers more quantities of goods to a lesser quantities.
4. The consumer is rational and transitive.
5. There is ordinal measurement of utility.
6. There is perfect divisibility of the goods under consideration.

Properties or Characteristics of Indifference Curve Analysis

The following are the properties of Indifference curve analysis.

I. Indifference curve slopes downwards from left to right. Indifference curve always slopes downward from left to right because of the law of substitution. According to the law of substitution the consumer goes on substituting a commodity which yields more satisfaction to a commodity which yields less satisfaction to get maximum total satisfaction.

On OX axis commodity 'X' is represented. On OY axis commodity 'Y' is represented. IC is a downward sloping Indifference Curve, the consumer selects a combination of OE of commodity 'Y' and OM of commodity 'X'. If a consumer want to acquire more of commodity 'X' (MN) he has to forego some units of commodity 'Y' (EF). Hence the IC slopes downwards.

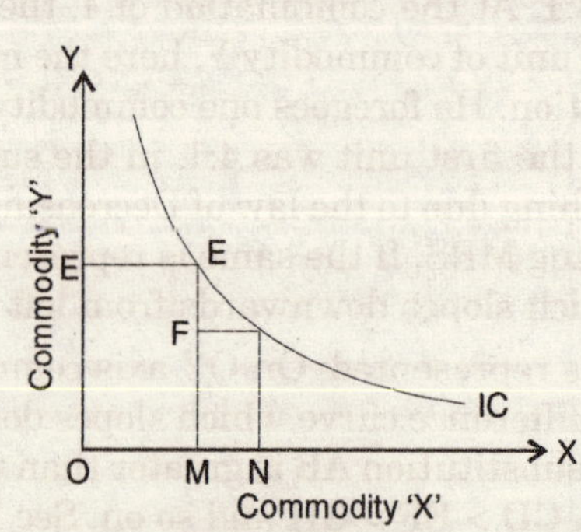

Fig. 2.5

There are some impossible (unusual) Indifference Curves, this is due to:

(*a*) ***If a consumer purchases only commodity 'X':*** If a consumer purchases only commodity 'X' then the indifference curve is horizontal straight line to OX axis. Which is shown diagrammatically as follows.

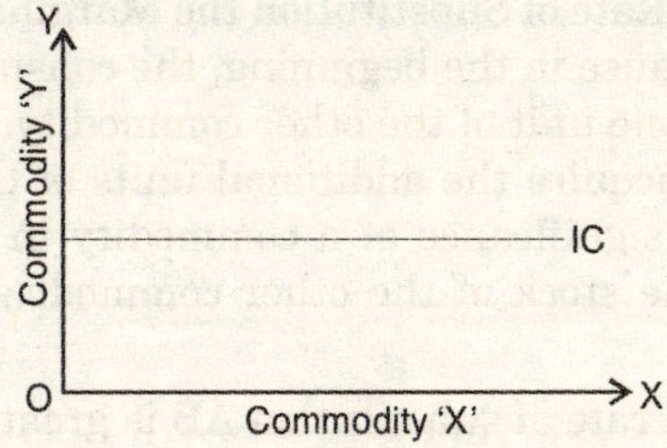

Fig. 2.6

(*b*) **If a consumer purchases only commodity 'Y'.** If a consumer purchases only commodity 'Y' then the Indifference curve is vertical to OX axis. Which is shown diagrammatically in Fig. 2.7.

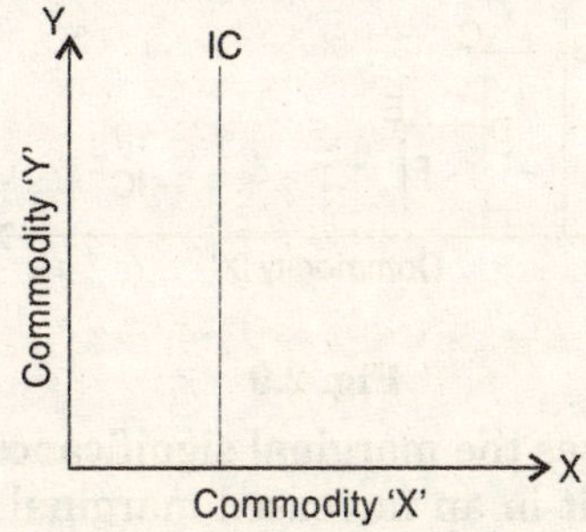

Fig. 2.7

(*c*) ***If a consumer increases the purchases of both the commodities:*** if a consumer increases the purchases of both the commodities then indifference curve slopes upward from left to right. Which is shown diagrammatically as follows. Thus (*a*) and (*b*) are not indifference curves where as (*c*) best suits the IC per se.

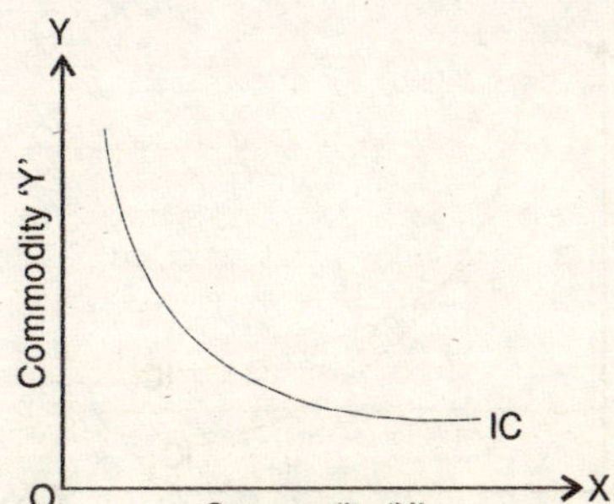

Fig. 2.8

II. The indifference curve is always convex to the origin. The indifference curve is always convex to the origin point 'O', because of the law of Diminishing Marginal Rate of Substitution. According to the law of marginal rate of substitution, in order to get the same level of total satisfaction, if the consumer purchases more of one commodity, he foregoes some units of another commodity. According to the Law of Diminishing Marginal Rate of Substitution the Marginal Rate of Substitution goes on decreasing. This is because in the beginning, the consumer may offer more units of a commodity to acquire one unit of the other commodity. But at a later stage, he offers less and less units to acquire the additional units of the other commodity this is so because the marginal significance of a commodity in terms of the other decreases with an increase in the stock of the other commodity. This we can observe in the figure.

In the figure the marginal rate of substitution AB is greater than CD and CD is greater than EF which is AB>CD>EF etc.

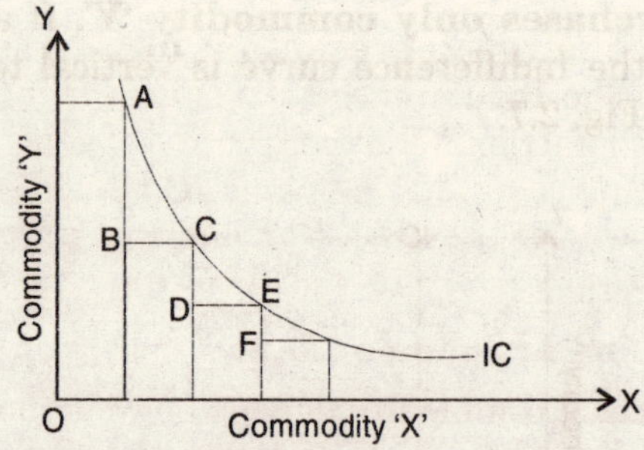

Fig. 2.9

It is argued that in some cases the marginal significance of a commodity in terms of the other may increase. This will result in an increased marginal rate of substitution. But this is only a temporary phenomenon. If the MRS increases then the AB is lesser than CD, CD is lesser than EF and so on. Which is AB < BC < EF etc., here the IC is conclave to the origin.

III. Two ICs cannot intersect each other. The two indifference curves cannot intersect each other because each indifference curve represents different levels of satisfaction. We never get a common point representing equal level of satisfaction of both the indifference curves.

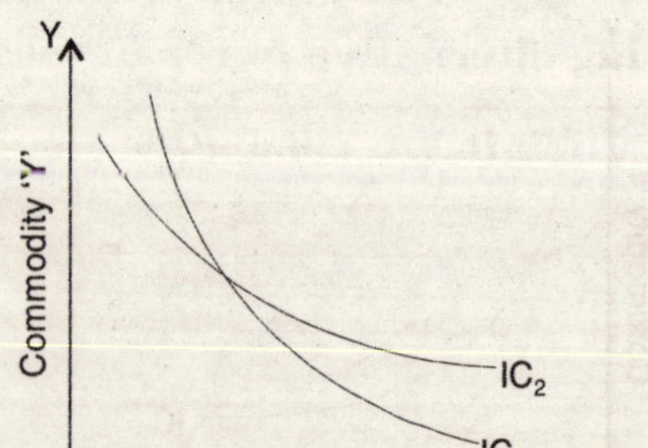

Fig. 2.10

IV. Need not be parallel. Indifference Curves on the Indifference Map need not necessarily be parallel to each other because of different MRS at different IC curves.

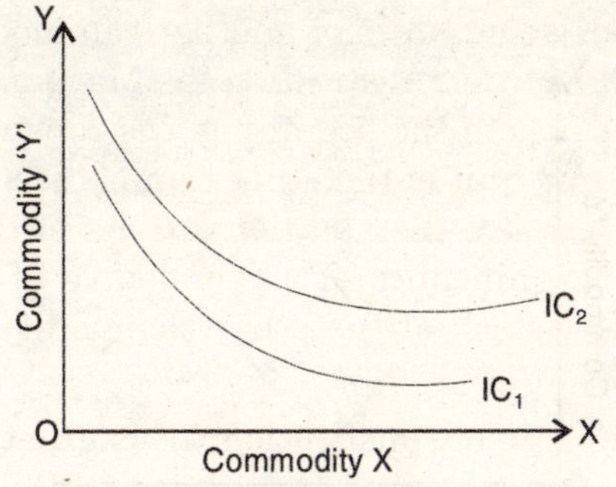

Fig. 2.11

V. Higher indifference curve represents a higher level of satisfaction. If the Indifference curve in the Indifference Map is at a higher level, it represents higher degree of level of satisfaction. The Indifference curve below shows less degree of satisfaction when compared to the previous IC to a consumer, hence in the process, the rational consumer prefers higher IC s but it is ultimately guided by the amount available for consumption.

The Budget Line or Price Line or Income Line

The consumer demand for a commodity depends on his money income and price of the commodity. Thus the income and prices are the two objective factors which form the budgetary constraint of the consumer. Let us assume that the consumer has an income of Rs. 50 to be spent on two goods X and Y. The price of X is Rs. 5 per unit and the price of Y is Rs 10 per unit. Then the consumer has three alternatives to spend

(*a*) He can spend entire Rs. 50 on the purchase of commodity 'X' alone so that he can purchase 10 units of it, or,

(*b*) He can spend entire Rs 50 on the purchase of commodity 'Y' so that he can buy 5 units, or

(*b*) He can spend Rs. 50 on the combinations of both the commodities as given in Table 2.7.

Table 2.7

Table showing alternative purchase possibilities

Alternative purchase possibilities	*Units of commodity 'Y'*	*Units of commodity 'X'*
A	5	0
	4	2
	3	4
	2	6
	1	8
B	0	10

It is clear that the consumer can spend his given income on any one of the alternative combinations of two goods X and Y. He can have an infinite number of purchase combinations of X and Y as represented in a figure.

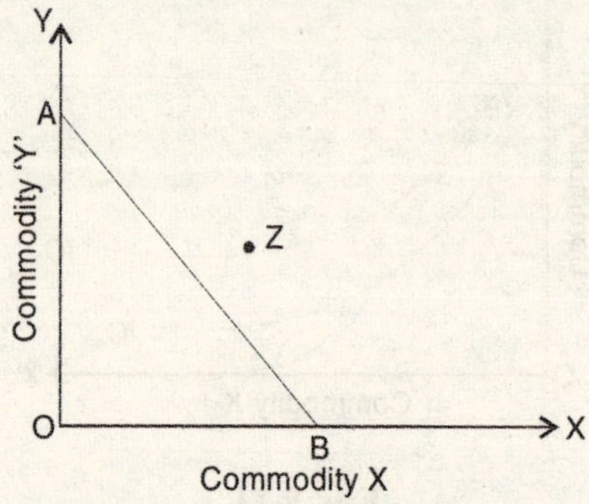

Fig. 2.12

If consumer spends his entire income on commodity 'Y' he can buy to the extent of OA or if he spends his entire income on commodity 'X' he can buy to the extent of OB. By joining AB we derive a line or curve called AB, which is a budget or income line, which represents various combinations of two goods he can buy. The consumer cannot go beyond this point or to point 'Z' because he can buy only combinations of these goods out of his limited income. To reach point Z he should increase the budget of income.

Definition: *The Budget line is the locus of points representing all the combinations of the two goods that can be purchased by the consumer, with his limited money income and given prices of the goods.*

The Consumer Equilibrium through Indifference Curves

A rational consumer attains an equilibrium position when his motive of maximizing satisfaction is realized. Under this approach, the assumption is that the consumer tries to maximize satisfaction, but it doesn't mean that maximization of satisfaction means achieving the maximum total utility but it is also reaching the higher level of satisfaction.

The consumer equilibrium is possible only by considering the following **assumptions.** They are:

1. The consumer has a fixed amount of income to spend.
2. He intends to buy a combination of two goods X and Y.
3. The prices of both the commodities are given and are constant.
4. Each of the commodities commodity 'X' and commodity 'Y' is homogeneous and divisible.
5. The consumer has definite tastes and preferences.
6. The consumer is rational.

To explain the consumers' equilibrium through indifference curves, we should consider the scale of preference that is, indifference map and the budget line or price line. The indifference map is a set of indifference curves, each indifference curve represents different level of satisfaction. Higher the indifference curve, higher is the level of satisfaction and lower the level of indifference curve, lower will be the level of satisfaction. The consumer always intends to have higher indifference curve but his activities (preferences of commodities) are guided by his money income also. The price line or budget line shows the various combinations of two goods that the consumer can buy with his given income at the existing prices. He cannot go beyond this price line AB.

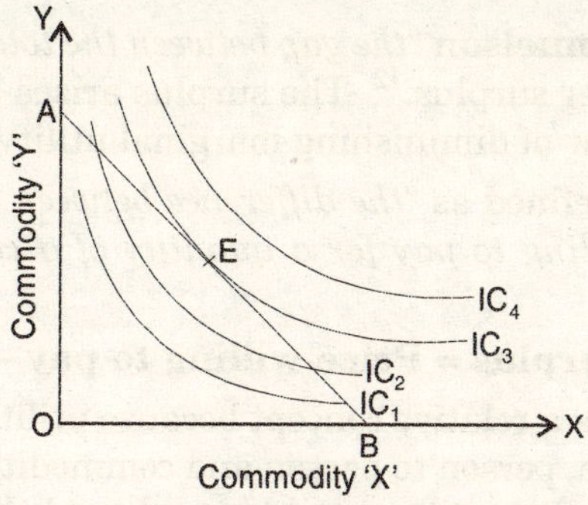

Fig. 2.13

In this diagram the consumer is in equilibrium at point 'E' where IC_3 is tangent to price line and this point is convex to the origin 'O'. The consumer will not get maximum satisfaction from IC_1 and IC_2, because his level of satisfaction is less with his income and he cannot opt IC_4, since his level of satisfaction is more but his income is limited to AB and he cannot go behind this. Hence the consumer is in equilibrium at a point E where IC is tangent to price line and it should be convex to the origin.

CONSUMER'S SURPLUS

The study of consumers surplus is more relevant to any organisation especially to a marketing manager who is involved in the process of knowing the value of the product manufactured, its capacity to fulfill the needs and requirements of the consumer, pricing strategy and price discrimination in the market. [11]This law is also more relevant to the producers to know the producer surplus, which is "*the difference between the price at which producers would have been willing to supply a good and the price they actually receive*". This law is also helpful to the government to evaluate its various decisions. For example, the NDA government at the union government took a decision to construct quadrilateral national highways from north to south and east to west of 14,000 kms. This decision will definitely decrease the cost of operation and maintenance expenses of the users of these roads. Naturally this decision will increase the value which the consumers of these roads never expected. This is evaluating it as a good decision. Similarly the decision taken by the Government of Karnataka to build fly overs, under bridges, Bangalore Metro rail project etc., to decongest the Bangalore City and to reduce pollution, operating cost of transport is also such an example.

Originally a French engineer-economist Arsene Jules Dupuit invented the doctrine of Consumer's surplus in 1844. Later it was popularized into economic theory by Alfred Marshall, hence it is popularly called as ***Marshallian Consumer's Surplus.***

[11] David C.Colander, "Economics" Irwin/Mc Graw-Hill, international edition, p. 611.

Definitions

According to *Prof. Alfred Marshall* consumer's surplus refers to *"Excess of the price that the consumer is willing to pay for a commodity rather than going without it over what he actually does pay"*.

According to **Paul A. Samuelson** *"the gap between the total utility of a good and its total market value"* is called consumer surplus.[12] The surplus arises because we *"receive more than we pay for"* as a result of the law of diminishing marginal utility.

Consumer's Surplus is defined as *"the difference between the total amount of money the consumer would have been willing to pay for a quantity of a commodity and the amount he actually had to pay for it"*.

Therefore **Consumer Surplus = Price willing to pay – Actual price paid.**

The consumer's surplus is a relative concept because utility is a relative term. Consumer surplus varies from time to time, person to person and commodity to commodity. The consumer surplus is found in some commodities like matchbox, salt and the like.

The following Table 2.7 shows the measurement of Consumer surplus.

Table 2.7

Measurement of consumer surplus

Units of commodity 'X'	*Marginal utility (in units)*	*Market price (one Rs. = one units)*	*Consumer surplus (in units)*
1	35	10	25
2	30	10	20
3	25	10	15
4	10	10	0
Total	**100**	**40**	**60**

The above table shows that the consumer is willing to pay to the extent of his marginal utility he derives from this product. The above table shows that the consumer is willing to pay Rs. 35 (to the extent of marginal utility), but it is available in the market for Rs. 10 for first unit of commodity X hence the consumer surplus is 25 units. Similarly for the second and third units the marginal utility derived decreases to 30 and 25 because of the law of DMU, hence he gets consumer surplus of 20, 15 units. From the last unit he gets zero consumer surplus, because the marginal utility and market price are equal. The total consumer surplus from the purchase of all the four units is 100, and the total market price paid is Rs. 40 and the total consumer surplus is 60 units.

Diagrammatic Representation of Consumer Surplus

The units of commodity are represented on OX-axis and price and marginal utility are represented on OY-axis. MU is a marginal utility curve or demand curve, which slopes downward from left to right. The total utility, the consumer gets from all of his units of commodity or price he is willing to pay is OMRQ. The total market price at which it is available in the market is for OPRM hence consumers surplus is OMRQ – OPRM = PQR or the shaded area.

[12] Paul A. Samuelson and William D. Nordhaus, "Economics", Tata McGraw-Hill publishing company Limited, New Delhi, p. 91.

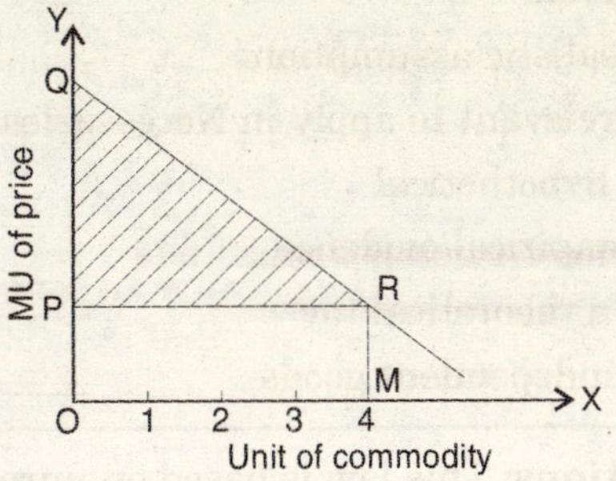

Fig. 2.14

Assumptions

The law is based on the following assumptions.

Assumptions
1. Cardinal measurement of utility
2. Ceteris peribus
3. Law of DMU
4. Constant MU of money
5. No substitutes
6. Specificity of utility

1. **Cardinal measurement of utility.** It is assumed that the utility derived by the consumer is measurable in terms of units. For example the utility derived from gel pen is 20 units, Reynolds pen is 10 units etc.
2. **Ceteris Paribus.** The Law assumes only one commodity with which we are dealing. Other commodities remain constant.
3. **Diminishing marginal utility.** This law assumes the concept of law of D.M.U. the consumer stops purchasing good when marginal utility of a commodity is equal to price.
4. **Constant marginal utility of money.** This law assumes that marginal utility of money remains constant throughout the process of exchange. In other words, the quantities of money paid for a commodity are assumed to be proportional to the quantities of satisfaction derived.
5. **No substitutes.** Marshall assumes that the commodity in question has no substitutes. If there are substitutes, the consumer will shift to purchase the other commodity as soon as marginal utility decreases or equals the price.
6. **Specificity of utility.** Marshall assumed that utility of a commodity depends specifically on the quantity of that commodity alone.

Criticisms against Consumer's Surplus

The economists like Cannan, Nicholson, Robinson and Davenport have criticized the concept of consumer's surplus. Some of the issues raised are:

Criticisms
1. Unrealistic assumptions
2. Not relevant to apply in Necessaries of life
3. It is hypothetical
4. No empirical evidence
5. It is a theoretical toy
6. Not independent goods

1. **Unrealistic assumptions:** This law is based on unrealistic assumptions like utility can be measured cardinally, marginal utility of money remains constant and the like.
2. **Necessaries of life:** It is meaningless to apply the doctrine of consumer surplus to necessity of life because in the case of necessity of life like water, the consumer derives infinite utility and would be willing to pay anything he can rather than go without it. For example in cities like Bangalore we are ready to pay Rs. 3000 for a square feet of land. Hence the consumer surplus in the case of necessaries of life is infinite.
3. **Hypothetical and Illusionary:** The concept of C S is hypothetical and illusionary because this does not exist in reality. Whatever the price is available in the market he must accept.
4. **No empirical evidence:** Marshall did not provide a data or empirical evidence in support of this concept. It is purely subjective phenomenon, not capable of empirical testing.
5. **Theoretical:** The study of C S is a useless theoretical toy, having no practical significance according to Prof. M.I.D Little. Marginal utility of money cannot be constant because if we spend more on one commodity, less money is available for other goods naturally the utility of money will increase. The absence of substitutes in the market is also impossible.
6. **Not independent goods:** The assumption of different units of the commodity has different utilities. The utility of each commodity is regarded as something independent.

Importance of this Law

Though this law is criticised on several grounds, it has some theoretical and practical significance. They are.

Importance
1. Clarifies the paradox of value
2. Useful to the finance minister
3. Useful to the monopolist
4. Comparing standard of living
5. Measuring capital gains in international trade

1. **It clarifies the paradox of value.** the concept of consumer's surplus is useful in clarifying the paradox of value by showing distinction between value in use and value in exchange. Paradox of value may be seen in the market value of some commodities like diamond and water. Water has immense value-in-use but little price or value in

exchange, while diamond has high value-in-exchange but low value in usefulness. Scarce marginal utility increases the price. If the marginal utility decreases the price also decreases. Now a days mineral water offers the role of value in exchange. This is the paradigm shift.

2. **Useful to the finance minister.** This doctrine is very much useful to the finance minister to impose taxes on the basis of consumer surplus. The consumer's surplus is a determining factor to the finance minister for levying taxes he can charge more taxes on the commodities from which the consumers surplus is more and vice versa. For instance in 1980s the tax was not imposed on ice cream. But the State Finance Minister observed that the consumer surplus derived from the ice cream is more hence they charged more taxes by the state governments. Similar in case of Fringe Benefit Tax. The present Finance Minister observed that the consumer surplus is more among the employees, who are getting more fringe benefits. They are willing to pay for the commodities is increasing due to increase in salary and fringe benefits when compared to the other class of people, hence he felt it is judicious to tax them.
3. **Useful to the monopolist.** The monopolist can charge the price of his good based on the law of consumer surplus. He charges more prices when consumer surplus is more. For example beauty parlors located in five star hotels charge more price than the price in the market, because they knew that the CS deriving by their consumers is more.
4. **For comparing standard of living.** The standard of living of the people can be measured on the basis of consumer surplus. If the consumer surplus of the people of that country is high, it indicates that they are expecting to pay more for the commodity than what actually they pay.
5. **For measuring gains in international trade.** People import goods through which they get more consumers surplus. If the commodities are imported from the other country, it indicates that the consumer surplus is more and the gain from international trade is more than purchasing same type of good in the domestic market.

People import goods from the consumer surplus oriented countries and thereby they make gain out of the global trade on the basis of excess surplus gained.

SUPERIORITY OF INDIFFERENCE CURVE TECHNIQUE OVER MARSHALLIAN APPROACH

The Indifference Curve technique is superior to the marshallian utility analysis in several ways.

Superiority of indifference curve technique

1. IC is more realistic measurement of utility
2. No assumption that the marginal utility of money remains constant
3. Analysis of multi-goods model
4. IC analysis provides better classification of coods into substitutes and complements

5. IC Analysis explain the law of DMU without the unrealistic assumption of the utility analysis
6. IC analysis explain the dual effect of the price effect.
7. IC analysis explain the law of demand more realistically
8. IC analysis explain the proportionality rule in a better way

1. **IC is more realistic measurement of utility.** The Indifference Curve technique assumes ordinal measurement of utility by which the consumer need not assign exact numerical numbers to represent the amount of utility attributable to the various units of the commodity. But the consumer must be in a position to judge whether one level of satisfaction is equal to, lower than, or higher than, the other or scale of preference.

2. **No assumption that the marginal utility of money remains constant.** The Marshallian utility theory is based on the assumption of the constant marginal utility of income. It means that the change in the income of the consumer does not affect his purchases. The indifference curve technique does not make use of these unrealistic assumptions. On the other hand, it clearly explains the income effect. It points out as to how consumer's purchases change with the change in his income.

3. **Analysis of multi-goods model.** Marshall in his utility analysis confines precisely to single good model by assuming the utility or demand for one good is independent of the other good and the marginal utility of money remains constant. But indifference curve technique analyse precisely the multi–good model and therefore it explains the relationship of substitution and complementary. This facilitates inter-commodity analysis, which is so significant in the price analysis.

4. **IC Analysis provides better classification of goods into substitutes and complements.** The classical economists explained substitutes and complements in terms of cross elasticity of demand, whereas in Indifference curves, hicks explains them after making compensating variation in income through Income substitution and cross substitution.

5. **IC Analysis explain the law of diminishing marginal Utility without the unrealistic assumption of the utility analysis.** Under utility analysis the Law of DMU is explained with reference to all types of goods including money. Whereas in the IC analysis it is replaced by the Law of Diminishing Marginal Rate of Substitution, which is scientific and also relieves us from psychological quantitative measurements of the utility analysis.

6. **IC Analysis explain the dual effect of the price effect.** The Marshallian Utility analysis fails to analyze income and substitution effects with the change in price. Whereas under IC analyses the impact of fall in price on the income and also on the substitution is clearly explained.

7. **IC Analysis explain the law of demand more realistically.** Under Indifference curve anlysis the law of demand is explained more realistically with more than one way. For example Indifference curve anlysis explains the situation of Giffen's goods in two ways. a) With the fall in price of inferior goods the demand remains unchanged because, income effect exactly equals substitution effect. b) When the price of the commodity falls, its demand also falls because in case of inferior goods income effect outweighs the substitution effect.

8. **IC analysis explain the proportionality rule in a better way.** According IC technique the consumer is in equilibrium at a point when his budget line is tangent to the indifference curve, at this point the slope of the IC equals the budget line, so that the

$$\text{MRS of X for Y} = \frac{\text{Price of X}}{\text{Price of Y}}$$

According to Marshalls proportionate rule, the consumer is in equilibrium when the

$$\frac{\text{MU of X}}{\text{Price of X}} = \frac{\text{MU of Y}}{\text{Price of Y}}$$

QUESTIONS ON THE CHAPTER

(Two marks)

1. What do you mean by Consumers' Sovereignty? Distinguish between opportunities and consumer preferences with a recent example.
2. Mention the approaches in the study of consumer behavior.
3. What is meant by cardinal approach?
4. What do you mean by ordinal approach?
5. What is meant by utility?
6. What do you mean by Total utility?
7. What is Law of Substitution?
8. What do you mean by law of Maximum Satisfaction?
9. What do you mean by law of Equi-Marginal Returns?
10. Define the law of Equi-Marginal Utility.
11. What is Marginal Utility?
12. What is meant by Ceteris Paribus.
13. What is Scale of Preference?
14. What is meant by Indifference Schedule?
15. What is Indifference curve?
16. What is Indifference Map?
17. What do you mean by MRS?
18. Why there is Diminishing MRS in Indifference Curve?
19. What is Budget Line?
20. What is Consumer Surplus?
21. Mention the goods or services from which you get Consumer Surplus.

(Five marks)

1. How is the Consumers' Sovereignty is manifested in a capitalistic economy?
2. Is consumer's sovereignty desirable? Explain.

3. Distinguish between Utility and Satisfaction.

4. Explain the law of Equi-marginal utility with the help of a diagram.

5. What is Indifference Curve? Mention the properties of IC.

6. Explain the Budget Line in IC with an example.

7. On what grounds do you say that cardinal approach to consumer's equilibrium is unrealistic?

8. Explain the doctrine of Consumer Surplus with the help of suitable example and a diagram.

Essay Type Questions (Fifteen marks)

1. Define consumers' sovereignty. Explain the limitations of consumers sovereignty

2. Explain the law of Equi- marginal utility with empirical evidence.

3. State and explain the law of Equi-Marginal Utility.

4. State and explain the law of Diminishing Marginal Utility and discuss the various exceptions to the law.

5. What are indifference curves? Discuss the various properties of Indifference curves with the help of diagrams.

6. Explain the Indifference Curve Analysis?

7. What is IC? Explain the properties of IC.

8. Explain the consumer's equilibrium through indifference curve technique.

9. Critically evaluate the law of Consumer Surplus.

10. What is consumer's surplus/ explain its criticisms and practical importance.

PRACTICAL PROBLEM

1. *Using the following schedule, show how the consumer maximizes utility.*

Units of commodities	*Price of commodity 'A'*	*Marginal utility of commodity 'A'*	*Price of commodity 'B'*	*Marginal utility of commodity 'B'*
1	2	30	4	40
2	2	18	4	32
3	2	16	4	28
4	2	8	4	24
5	2	6	4	20

Solution. A consumer maximises utility when,

$$\frac{\text{Marginal utility of commodity X}}{\text{Price of commodity X}} = \frac{\text{Marginal utility of commodity Y}}{\text{Price of commodity Y}}$$

By using this formula, the consumer attains equilibrium or maximizes utility.

Units of commodites	*Price of commodity 'A'*	*Marginal utility of 'A'*	*MU of A / price of commodity 'A'*	*Price of commodity 'B'*	*Marginal utility of 'B'*	*MU of B / price of commodity 'B'*
1	2	30	30/2 = 15	4	40	40/4 = 10
2	2	18	18/2 = 9	4	32	32/4 = 8
3	2	16	**16/2 = 8**	4	28	28/4 = 7
4	2	8	8/2 = 4	4	24	24/4 = 6
5	2	6	6/2 = 3	4	20	20/4 = 5

The consumer gets maximum satisfaction by purchasing 3 units of commodity A and 2 units of commodity B, where the marginal utilities of last unit of money spends tend to equal *i.e.,* 8

2. *Given the following utility schedules show how a consumer should allocate the budget of Rs. 5 so that he maximises utility.*

Expenditure	*Marginal*	*Utility of expenditure (Rs.)*
Rs.	*good A*	*good B*
1	80	50
2	60	40
3	40	30
4	20	25
5	10	15

Solution. Consumer attains equilibrium, when he gets maximum satisfaction out of his Rs. 5.

There are three alternatives to this

One, he can spend entire Rs. 5 on Good 'A' so he gets total MUE is 210.

Second, he can spend entire Rs. 5 on Good 'B' so he gets total MUE of 160

Third, the combination of both the goods. the various combinations are

(*a*) Rs. 4 on Good A + Rs. 1 on Good B = Rs. 250

(*b*) Rs. 3 on Good A + Rs. 2 on Good B = Rs. 270

(*c*) Rs. 2 on Good A + Rs. 3 on Good B = Rs. 260

(*d*) Rs. 1 on Good A + Rs. 4 on Good B = Rs. 225

Ans. Consumer attains equilibrium when he spends Rs. 3 on Good A and Rs. 2 on Good B, he gets maximum satisfaction of Rs. 270.

EXERCISE PROBLEM

1. Given the following utility schedules show how a consumer should allocate the budget of Rs. 5 so that he maximizes utility.

Expenditure	*Marginal Utility of expenditure (Rs.)*	
Rs.	*Good A*	*Good B*
1	15	14
2	14	13
3	13	12
4	12	11
5	11	10

PRACTICAL PROBLEMS ON CONSUMERS SURPLUS

1. *Using the following data, calculate consumers' surplus for each unit and give a graphic representation.*

Commodity bought	*Price in Rs.*	*Total utility in Rs.*
1	50	85
2	50	80
3	50	75
4	50	70
5	50	50

(Bangalore University I Semester B.Com Nov/Dec 2004)

Solution. ***Formula to calculate consumers' surplus***

C.S = Total utility (price willing to pay) – Actual Price

Statement showing the computation of Consumers' Surplus

Commodity bought	*Price in Rs.*	*Total utility in Rs.*	*Consumers' surplus*
1	50	85	35
2	50	80	30
3	50	75	25
4	50	70	20
5	50	50	0
Total	250	360	110

Consumer Surplus = Total Utility – Total Price

= 360 – 250 = 110

Graphical representation of Consumers' Surplus

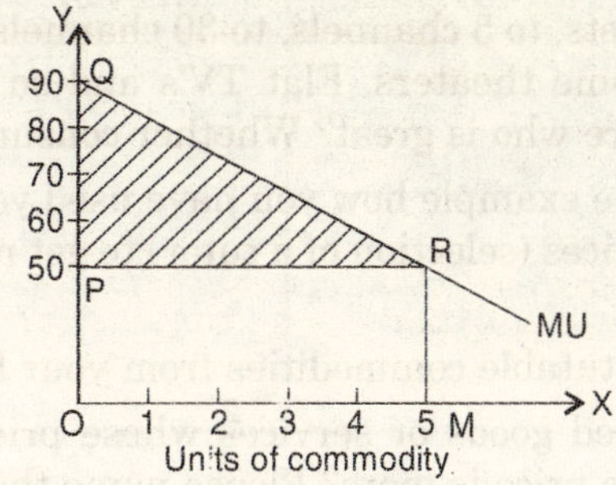

Fig.

Total Price = Rs. 250 or OPRM

Total Utility = Rs. 360 or OQRM

Consumer Surplus = T.U. – T.P.

= Rs. 360 – Rs. 250 = Rs. 110

OR

= OQRM – OPRM = PQR

EXERCISE PROBLEM

1. Using the following data, calculate consumers' surplus for each unit.

Commodity bought	*Price in Rs.*	*Total utility in Rs.*
1	30	65
2	30	50
3	30	45
4	30	30
5	30	20

SKILL DEVELOPMENT

1. List the products for which consumer doesn't have freedom in selection of his products.
2. List the services for which consumer doesn't have freedom in selection.
3. Identify some products or services pricing in India are not with the intention of satisfying consumers'.
4. Add some more factors of limitations to the consumers' sovereignty.
5. Your father gets you a bike of your choice, as an incentive for securing distinction in Pre-University exams. Here identify who is a customer and who is a consumer.
6. There are two choices one is you can buy a motor bike manufactured by 'X' manufacturer without any market survey and another is a 'Y' manufacturer manufactures motor bike identifying the preferences in color, design, requirements and so on after conducting market survey. Which one of these will you buy.

7. The TV manufacturing companies first manufactured white and block TV sets then they changed to color sets, to 5 channels, to 30 channels, to 60 channels, 99 channels, remote controllers, Home theaters, Flat TV's and so on to whom? Why there are changing like this? Here who is great? Whether consumer or manufacturer.
8. From your own life time example how you have used your limited money in selection of books (goods) or services (selection of a tutor) to get maximum satisfaction prepare an illustration.
9. Prepare a list of substitutable commodities from your life experience.
10. Have you ever preferred goods or services whose prices are less to substitute the goods or services whose price is more? Please name them.
11. Have you or your parents ever substituted a scarce good or service. If so which goods or services. Please discuss this with your friends.
12. Have you ever been acted as irrational consumer? Why. Discuss the conditions.
13. Have you experienced getting maximum satisfaction in exchanging Indian goods mentally with the goods made in China? If so guide your Indian manufacturer about your expectations in the product.
14. Construct one illustration for the Law of Equi-Marginal Utility from your imaginary figures.
15. Draw a diagram representing the law of Equi-Marginal Utility.
16. Consult your parents and prepare a budget of your family for one month. Then take the same amount of budget and allocate your expenses in the another month of festival or a family function and observe the process of substitution of one commodity for another commodity or commodities within the same amount of the budget.
17. Prepare a scale of preference to join a college from the group of colleges available from the neighboring places.
18. Prepare an imaginary combination of two goods or services, which gives you same level of satisfaction.
19. Plot the diagrams for each of the properties of Indifference Curve Analysis.
20. List the products for which you are ready to pay more than its price.
21. Advice your Finance Minister by identifying some of the products in your day to day life for which you are ready to pay more. So that it will help him to levy more taxes.
22. From the imaginary example construct an illustration showing consumers surplus and draw a diagram showing consumer surplus.

CHAPTER

3

THEORY OF DEMAND AND ANALYSIS

CHAPTER OUTLINE	LEARNING OBJECTIVES
— Demand in general and demand in Economics — Determinants of demand — Individual and market demand schedules — Law of demand — Assumptions — Exceptiosn to law of demand — Extension and contraction of demand — Increase and derease in demand — Elasticity of demand — Price, income, and cross — Price elasticity — Perfectly elastic — Perfectly inelastic — Relatively elastic — Relatively elastic — Relatively inelastic — Unitary elastic. — Factors influencing elasticity of demand — Practical significance of elasticity of demand — Measurement of price elaticity of demand — Total outlay method	After reading this chapter you should be able to : 1. Know the demand in general and in economics 2. Analyse the determinants of demand 3. Distinguish between individual and market demand schedules 4. Know the law of demand, its assumptions 5. Distinguish between extension and increase, contraction and decerase in demand. 6. Analyse elasticity of demand and its methods 7. Diagnose factors influencing demand. 8. Know the practical significance of elasticity of demand. 9. Know and understand how price elasticity is measured under total outlay method.

The demand for a product depends on various factors like price, income, prices of related products, population, availability of the products in the market, advertisement, climate, nature of economy, policy of the government, credit policy of the sellers, behaviour of the buyer, consumer tastes, preferences, and so on. These demand factors are not same for all the products but vary from one firm to the other and from product to product. Besides there are several other factors which are general in nature that determines the demand. The manager of a firm must know the factors, which determines the demand. The manager can identify and segregate factors into controllable factors and uncontrollable factors. Before going to the factors determining the demand, a brief look at some of the important concepts in demand analysis is essential.

MEANING OF DEMAND

In ordinary language *demand* means the desire for a commodity, desire to have a Toyota Corolla car, computer, washing machine, water cooler, dress materials and the like. In economics mere desire does not constitute demand. The desirer (the individual) must have necessary *purchasing* power and thereafter, he should show the *willingness* to buy. For instance, the desirer may have the money and desire to have a commodity or service, but that is not enough to constitute demand because he may even postpone the purchasing activity, hence economic principles insist on willingness to buy. Thus in economics **demand refers to the desire for a commodity backed by ability to pay and willingness to purchase at a certain price and at a particular time and in a particular market.**

It can be represented thus:

Demand = desire + purchasing power + willingness to buy

or

$$D = De + PP + WB$$

There is a close relationship between independent variable 'price' and dependent variable 'demand' and the relationship is expressed in the form of a law known as the law of demand. Which specify that there is indirect or inverse or opposite relationship between two factors price and demand.

Demand schedule. Demand Schedule refers to the list of different quantity demanded or purchased by the consumers at various prices. A demand schedule expresses the functional relationship between price and quantity demanded.

A demand schedule may be two types.

1. Individual demand schedule and
2. Market demand schedule

1. Individual demand schedule. Individual demand schedule refers to different quantities of commodity demanded at different prices by an individual consumer in the market. It can be shown in the form of table as follows

Table 3.1

Individual demand schedule

Price per unit of commodity X (in rupees)	*Quantity demanded (in kgs.)*
15	10
14	14
13	18
12	23
11	28
10	35

Table 3.1 reveals that when the price of a commodity X is Rs. 15 the quantity demanded is 10 kgs. When the price of a commodity decreases to Rs. 14, Rs. 13 and so on, the quantity demanded increases to 14 kgs, 18 kgs and so on. It indicates that when the price of a commodity decreases the quantity demanded by the consumer increases and vice versa.

2. Market Demand Schedule (MDS). Market demand schedules refer to the total quantity of a commodity purchased by all the consumers at different prices in a particular market. It can also be put that the market demand for a product is the sum of individual demand at a price per unit of time.

Market demand schedule can be calculated in two methods.

In one method, when the individual demand schedule of all the consumers in the market is totalled the market demand schedule is arrived at

In the second method, it is the individual demand schedule is multiplied by the total number of consumers in the market.

But in these two methods market demand schedule varies from the first method to the second method because of the variation in individual demand and the market demand schedule in the first method. Whereas in the second method it is presumed that all individuals demand and behave similarly, and MDS shows a different picture when compared to the first method.

As it is very difficult to add up the demand schedules of the entire unit of consumers in the market demand schedule by using the second method. The following is the imaginary market demand schedule, in which it is assumed that the number of consumers in the market demanding bananas is 1000. It can be shown in the form of a table.

Table 3.2. Market demand schedule

Price of bananas per kg (in Rs.)	*Quantity demanded by an average consumer (in kgs)*	*Number of consumers in the market (N = 1000)*	*Market demand per week (in kgs)*
10	1	1000	1000
8	2	1000	2000
6	4	1000	4000
4	7	1000	7000
2	10	1000	1000

When this demand schedule is represented in the form of a diagram, a curve called demand curve is obtained.

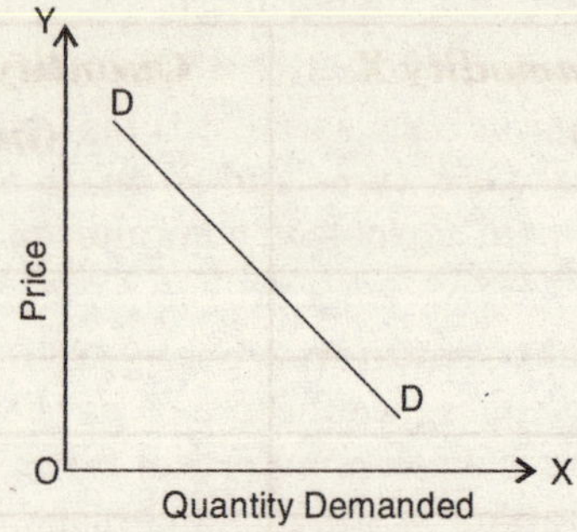

Fig. 3.1

In the above diagram the demand curve DD slopes negatively from left to right indicating that, with a fall in price, the demand tends to rise and with a rise in price the demand tends to fall. There is an inverse or opposite relationship between price and demand.

Demand Curve. The demand curve refers to the center of points on the diagram, which represents the quantity demanded in the market by all the consumers (in case of market demand) at different prices.

Market Demand Curve[1]. The curve indicates the total quantity or a good all consumers are willing and able to purchase at each possible price, holding the prices of related goods, income, advertising, and other variables constant.

Factors Influencing Demand
(Determinants of Demand)

There are various factors, which influence demand for a product. A closer look at these factors and analysis is worth to note.

Determinants of demand

1. Price of a commodity
2. Prices of related goods
3. Income of consumer
4. General price level
5. Change in population
6. Policy of the company
7. Technological changes
8. Weather and climate
9. Tastes, fashions and preferences
10. Government policy
11. Change in the distribution of income and wealth
12. Advertisement

[1] Michael R. Baye, '*Managerial Economics and Business Strategy*', Mc Graw-Hill International Edition, p-35.

1. **Price of a commodity.** The price of a commodity is one of the main factors that determine the demand. More quantities are demanded with lower price and fewer quantities are demanded at a higher price.
2. **Prices of related goods or substitutes or complementary goods.** The changes in the prices of related goods such as substitutes Coffee/Tea, Coke /Pepsi, LG/ Samsung T.V, Airtel/Hutch, MRF/ Ceat tyres and so on. In complementary goods and services like ink pen/ ballpoint pen, car/petrol, computer/printer, gas stove/gas also influence the demand for goods.
3. **Income of a potential consumer.** A change in income also significantly influences demand for goods. The aggregate income or per capita income or national income of the potential consumers is also an important factor which determines the demand for a product. The rise in income of the consumers increases the demand for a commodity in the market. For instance the increase in the income of government employees due to the implementation of fifth pay commission recommendations and UGC pay scales, the demand for small cars segment increased many fold and the number will increase further in future.
4. **The general price level.** The change in the general price level is also a factor which will have its impact on the demand for the goods and services. The increase in the general price level in an economy will decrease the real income of the consumers, hence the demand for a product in the market also decreases. For instance this situation normally happens in the post war period or post calamities period, hence the governments usually adopts its fiscal and monetary mechanism to correct this type of situations.
5. **Change in population of potential buyers.** The market demand for commodity substantially changed when there is a change in the total population. A larger number of buyers will constitute large demand and vice-versa. Thus growth of population is an important factor, a high growth of population over a period of time tends to imply a rising demand for essential goods and services in general. The MNCs such as coke, pepsi, and other FMCG sectors are inclined to operate in India because of its geographical area and population. For them the country is a fertile ground for lucrative businesses. Even if coke and pepsi each for example sell 25 crore bottles of soft drink per day at the profit rate of a rupee per bottle, they easily gain Rs. 25 crore each, that is why all MNCs vie for market access to India through WTO agreement.
6. **Institutional policies.** The credit policy of a company, after sales service, and customer relationship of a company will influence the demand for a product. The institutional policies brought a new dimension in the consumer's quality of service and consequentially that led to the increase in the demand for their goods and services. For instance the above services offered or facilitated by the automobile manufacturing companies boosted the demand for their vehicles in Indian market.
7. **Technological changes.** The anticipated technological changes of a product in an economy will determine the demand for the product. For instance when consumers expects that there will be change in the technology in future, immediately the demand for a product decreases. This can be observed in the electronic goods market like mobile phones.

8. **Weather and climate.** Demand for certain products are determined by weather and climatic conditions. For example, in summer there is a great demand for cool drinks, cool-joints products, similarly demand for hot and spicy junk foods during winter and great demand for rain coat and the like will be during rainy season in such a phenomenon.

9. **Tastes, fashions and preferences of the consumers.** The demand for a product is greatly affected by the change in the tastes, fashions and preferences of consumers. The scale of preference will have full play in fancy goods and fashionable articles. Example: Ganjam Nagappa and Tanishq for gold ornaments, ITC for apparels, Sunglasses, VOLVO for travelling, Nestle products and the like.

10. **Government policy.** The government policy of a country towards that particular product determines the demand. Eg., the exports of a product, regulations towards the quality of customer service etc.

11. **Change in the distribution of income and wealth.** If there is equal distribution of income and wealth in the society, the demand for many products and services of common consumption tends to be greater than in the case of unequal distribution. For example cellular and landline phones.

12. **Advertisement and sales propaganda.** Market demand for many products in the present day is influenced by seller efforts through advertisement in print and electronic media and sales propaganda which also affects consumers preferences.

Law of Demand

The law of demand states that ceteris paribus (other things remaining constant), *the quantity demanded extends with a fall in price and contracts with a rise in price*. In other words, this law states that *higher the price, lower the demand and lower the price higher the demand*. Thus this law indicates that there is an inverse relationship between price and demand.

$$LD = P\uparrow \ D\downarrow$$
$$P\downarrow \ D\uparrow$$

Assumptions of this law

Thr law of demand holds good only when the following assumptions are met, otherwise not. The presumptions or conjectures are.

1. The income of the people should remain constant.
2. The taste, fashions and preferences should remain constant.
3. Prices of related goods (substitutes and complementary) should remain constant.
4. The future price of the commodity should not change.
5. The commodity should not be one of prestige value articles or inferior ones.

The law of demand is explained in Table 3.2 for easy understanding. In law of demand the relationship is between price and demand. Price is the cause and demand is the effect. The relationship between two factors is opposite and if price goes upward, demand comes down and vice-versa.

Table 3.2

Table showing the relationship between price and demand (law of demand)

Price in Rs. *(Independent variable)*	*Demand (in kgs)* *(Dependent variable)*
5	10
4	20
3	30
2	40
1	50

When these figures are plotted on two axis OX and OY. The type of curve obtained is shown in Fig. 3.2

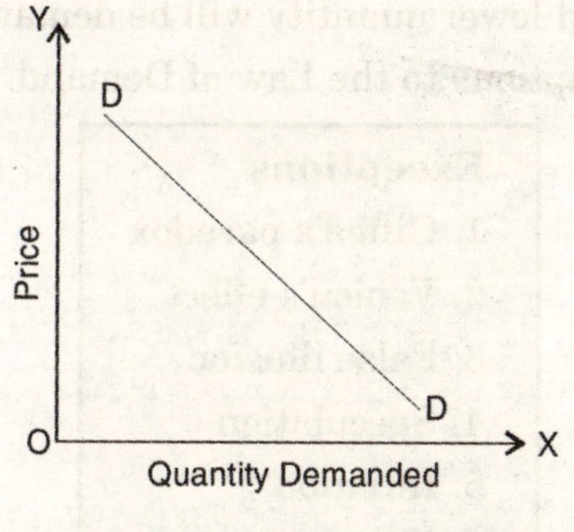

Fig. 3.2. Diagrammatic representation of law of demand

In the diagram OX axis represents the quantity demanded for commodity and OY axis represents the price of the commodity. DD is the demand curve which slopes downward from left to right. This downward sloping curve indicates that more will be demanded at a lower price and less will be demanded at a higher price.

Exceptions to the Law of Demand

Generally the law of demand states that there is an inverse relationship between price and quantity demanded, that is more of a commodity will be demanded at a lower price than at higher prices. But in certain cases the Law of Demand will not hold good, in such cases the demand curve will slope upward indicating higher demand at higher price and lower demand at lower price, this situation is called **exceptional demand.** It is an universal phenomenon that higher quantity will be demanded at lower prices, and lower will be demanded at higher prices and hence the demand curve always slopes downwards from left to right. If the demand curve slopes upwards from left to right indicating that higher quantity is demanded at higher prices and lower quantity will be demanded at lower price, then this demand curve is called **Exceptional Demand Curve.** This may be explained as under:

P↑ D↑

P↓ D↓

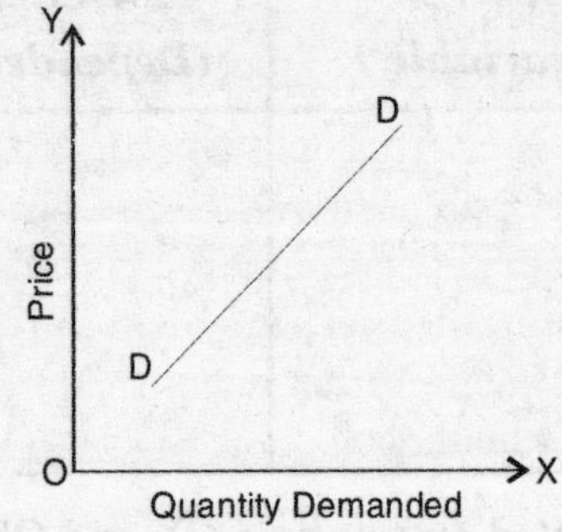

Fig. 3.3. Exceptional demand curve

Exceptional demand curve slopes upwards from left to right indicating that higher quantity is demanded at higher prices and lower quantity will be demanded at lower price.

The following are the exceptions to the Law of Demand.

Exceptions
1. Giffen's paradox
2. Veblon's effect
3. False illusion
4. Speculation
5. Inflation
6. Scarcity

1. **In case of inferior goods. (Giffen's goods or Giffen's paradox).** The law of demand is inoperative in case of certain necessities and inferior goods. People have to purchase necessaries of life, whatever may be the price. Generally poor people spend their income on inferior goods, even if the income of the people increases the demand for these goods remains constant or even decreases. Whenever the price of inferior goods falls the real income of the consumer will increase, with the help of this real income (savings or surplus out of price reduction) the consumer will purchase more of superior goods and less of inferior goods. This phenomenon was first observed by Robert Giffen, it is named after him as Giffen's paradox. According to him inferior good is 'potato' and superior good is 'meat' at Ireland. The Giffen's paradox holds that the demand is strengthened with a rise or weakened with a fall in price.
2. **In case of prestige value article. (Veblon's Effect, Snob Appeal).** The law of demand does not hold good in case of prestige value goods like diamond. People think that possession of more diamonds enhance their prestige in the society. If the price of diamond rises, the demand will be strengthened. Conversely people tend to cut their purchase when the price of demand falls. Professor Veblon calls this type of consumption as *conspicuous consumption. Eg., paintings, antiquities etc.*

3. **False Illusion. (Psychological bias).** Some people think that higher price means, higher quality and lower price means lower quality. Due to this psychological feeling people demand more at higher price and less at lower price. This is true in case of cosmetics and other articles of personal attraction. In Indian context silk saree, perfumes etc., are examples for such phenomenon.
4. **Future price. (Speculation).** If people anticipate that in future, price will be less than the present price, they will postpone the present consumption, as a result of this demand falls with a fall in price. On contrary, if people anticipate that in future, price will be higher than the present price, they will purchase more for the present at a higher price. This is due to expectation and speculation of the people. In such a case the law of demand will not hold good.
5. **Rise in price level. (Inflation).** During inflation prices of all commodities are on the rise, when the economy is experiencing hyper or galloping inflation, people will be keen to purchase more of essential goods, fearing that the prices may go up still further.
6. **Scarcity.** The law of demand does not operate when there is chronic shortage of commodities. During such times, in spite of increasing prices people will rush to buy fearing non-availability of goods. In case of essential goods also people will buy more quantities in the event of increase in prices.

EXTENSION AND CONTRACTION OF DEMAND

Changes (+ or –) in demand indicates extension and contraction of demand. If there is an increase in demand for a commodity or service due to fall in its own price, it is called *extension of demand* and when there is decrease in demand for commodity or service due to a rise in its price alone, it is called *contraction of demand.* In short, demand extends when the price falls and contracts when the price rises assuming that other things should remain constant. For example, the extension (+) and contraction (–) of demand for jeans pant due to its own fall or rise in price, by adhering to ceteris paribus principle.

Extension and contraction of demand indicates movement along the same demand curve. The consumer will have a fixed demand schedule in case of extension and contraction of demand. This can be explained in the form of a diagram (see Fig. 3.4)

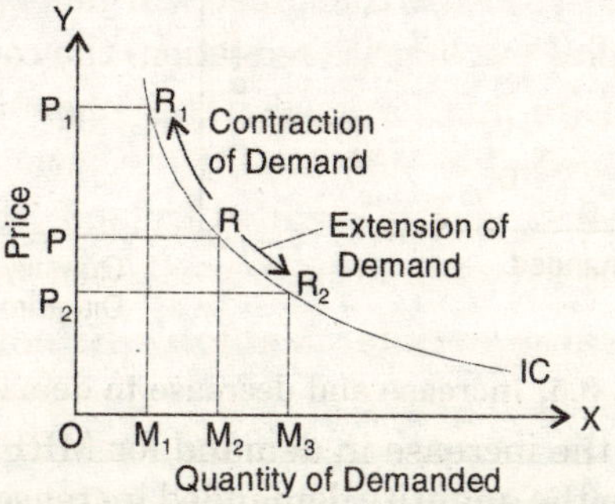

Fig. 3.4. Extension and Contraction of Demand

OP = Normal price

OM = Normal demand

Op_1 = Rise in price, R_1M_1 = Contraction of demand

OP_2 = Fall in price, R_2M_2 = Extension of demand

DD = Demand curve

$R_1 - R - R_2$ = Movements on the same demand curve

In the Fig. 3.4, OX axis represents the quantity demanded for jeans and OY axis represents the price of jeans. DD represents the demand curve. A downward movement from R to R_2 indicates extension of demand for jeans and upward movement from R to R_1 indicates contraction of demand. The points R, R_1 and R_2 represent the movements on the same demand curve DD. Thus whenever quantity demand changes due to a change in its own price of a commodity or service, such change is called extension and contraction of demand.

INCREASE AND DECREASE IN DEMAND

In case of increase and decrease in demand, the consumer changes the quantity demand not on account of changes in price of a commodity but due to changes in conditions or factors determining demand (other than price). The factors like changes in tastes, fashions, preferences, income, population, climatic conditions, technology, change in the price of related goods such as substitutes and complementary and the like.

If there is an increase in quantity demanded for factors other than price it is called *increase of demand.* Similarly, if there is less quantity demanded other than the factor price it is called *decrease of demand*. For example the change in demand for MRF tyres is not because of rise and fall in the prices of MRF tyres, but owing to change in the tastes, preferences, fashions, income of tyre users, technology, change in the prices of competitors like ceat and srichakra tyres of MRF tyres.

This increase and decrease in demand phenomenon is more fully explained in Fig. 3.5 diagrammatically.

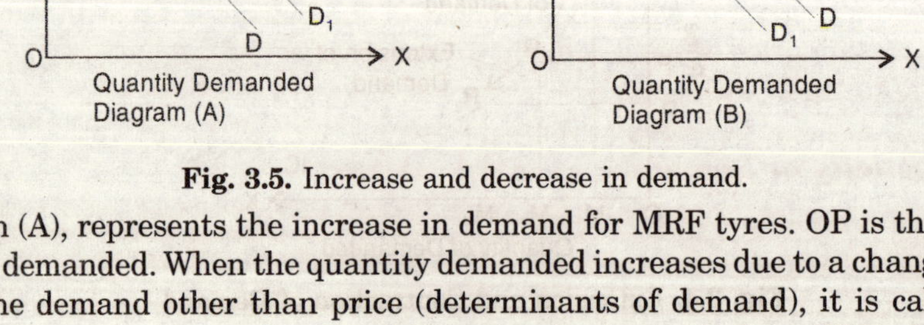

Fig. 3.5. Increase and decrease in demand.

Diagram (A), represents the increase in demand for MRF tyres. OP is the price and OM is the quantity demanded. When the quantity demanded increases due to a change in the factors determining the demand other than price (determinants of demand), it is called increase of demand. In this case, the demand curve shifts towards right side from DD to D_1D_1. Points RR, represent price of MRF tyres remaining unchanged.

Similarly, the diagram (B), represents the decrease in demand. Which is due to change in the conditions or factors influencing demand other than price. The shift of demand curve towards left side from DD to D_1D_1 is called decrease of demand. The points RR represent the price remaining unchanged.

The Extension and contraction, increase and decrease of demand are shown in the matrix for easy and simple understanding.

Matrix showing Extension, Contraction, Increase and Decrease of demand

Factors	Extension (+)	Contraction (–)	Increase (+)	Decrease (–)
Price of a commodity or service	Falls	Rises	No change	No change
Changes in tastes, preferences, fashions, technology	No influence on demand	No influence on demand	Influence on demand	Influence on demand
Prices of related goods (substitutes and Complementary)	Do not affect	Do not affect	Certainly affect the demand	Certainly affect the demand
Demand	Goes up	Comes down	Rises	Rises
Demand curve	One	One	Two	Two
Movements on the demand curve	Downward movement on the same demand curve	Upward movement on the same demand curve	Demand curve shifts towards right side	Demand curve shifts towards left side

ELASTICITY OF DEMAND

The law of demand explains the nature of relationship between demand and its determinants, but not the extent of relationship or responsiveness of demand with the change in its determinants. The nature of relationship between demand and its determinants is not merely sufficient to the manager or to the management to take decisions in their day to day business. The management must know the responsiveness or the degree of response of demand with the change in the price of the commodity change in the price of its substitutes, or change in the advertising policy, and as to what the response of the market is. It will become a basis for the manager to rise the price of his commodity when the cost of production increases or when selling or promotion expenses increase.

Meaning of Elasticity of Demand

The elasticity of demand is the degree or the rate of responsiveness of demand to a change in the determinants. In other words *elasticity of demand is the measure of the responsiveness of demand to the change in its determinants*. The degree of responsiveness of demand to the change in its determinants is called *elasticity of demand.*

Methods of Elasticity of Demand

There are three methods of elasticity of demand, they are

1. Price elasticity of demand
2. Income elasticity of demand and
3. Cross elasticity of demand.

Price Elasticity of Demand

Price elasticity of demand refers to the degree or level or extent of responsiveness / changes / sensitiveness of demand for a commodity or service to change in its price. The price elasticity of demand can be measured as:

$$Pe = \frac{\text{Proportionate change in quantity demand}}{\text{Proportionate change in price}}$$

In terms of symbols,

$$Pe = \frac{\Delta q}{q} / \frac{\Delta p}{p}$$

or

$$Pe = \frac{q}{q} \times \frac{p}{\Delta p}$$

Δq = change in quantity demanded

Δp = change in price.

Elasticity simply means change in quantity demand due to change in the commodity's or service's price for example the change in the demand for onion, edible oil, vegetables, petrol, gold and the like due to change in their respective price.

Elastic and Inelastic Demand

A change in demand is not always proportionate to the change in price. A small change in price may lead to a great change in demand which is called *elastic demand*. On the other hand, a big change in price leads to a small change in the quantity demanded which is called *inelastic demand*. Simply put:

Elastic: change in demand

Inelastic: No change in demand.

Types or Forms of price elasticity of demand

There are five types of price elasticity of demand. They are:

1. Perfectly elastic demand
2. Perfectly inelastic demand
3. Relatively elastic demand
4. Relatively inelastic demand
5. Unitary or unit elastic demand

1. **Perfectly elastic demand.** It refers to a situation where a small fall in price will result in infinite increase in the quantity demanded or small rise in price causes the quantity demand of the commodity to fall to zero. Hence in this case the demand curve can be shown as a horizontal straight line (see Fig. 3.6), symbolically Pe = ∝ (infinite), for example the gold prices in India

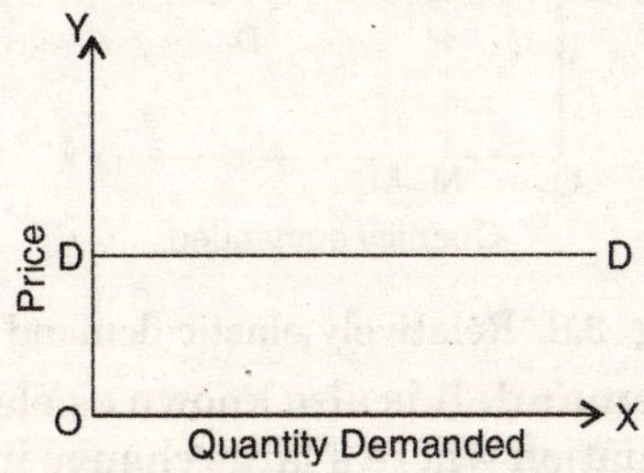

Fig. 3.6. Perfectly elastic demand

2. **Perfectly inelastic demand.** It refers to a situation where whatever may be change in the price level, same quantity will be demanded. For instance whatever may be price of a Newspaper, Salt, Matchbox, the quantity demanded will be more or less same. Hence in this case the demand curve can be shown as a vertical straight-line (see Fig. 3.7) where Pe = 0.

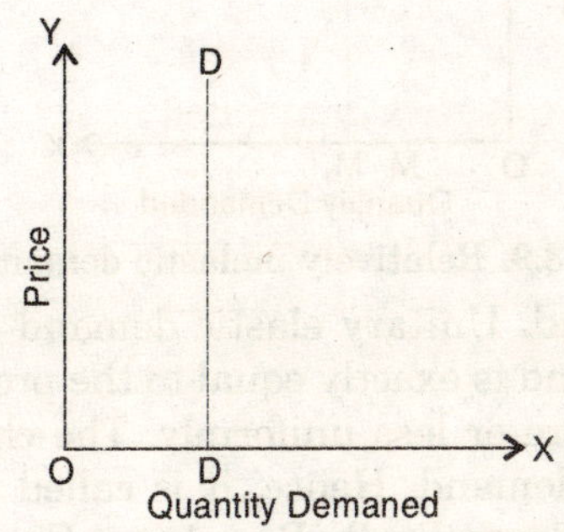

Fig. 3.7. Perfectly inelastic demand

3. **Relatively elastic demand.** It is also known as elasticity of demand greater than one (Pe > 1). It refers to a situation where a proportionate change in the quantity demand is greater or more than the proportionate change in the price of the commodity. Hence, it is called relatively (between demand and price relation) elasticity of demand or greater than unity or one. The demand curve will have flatter sloping, indicating the quantity demanded is larger to a change in price. In this case Pe > 1 (see Fig. 3.8). Example durable goods like Television sets, Motor cars, Air conditioners.

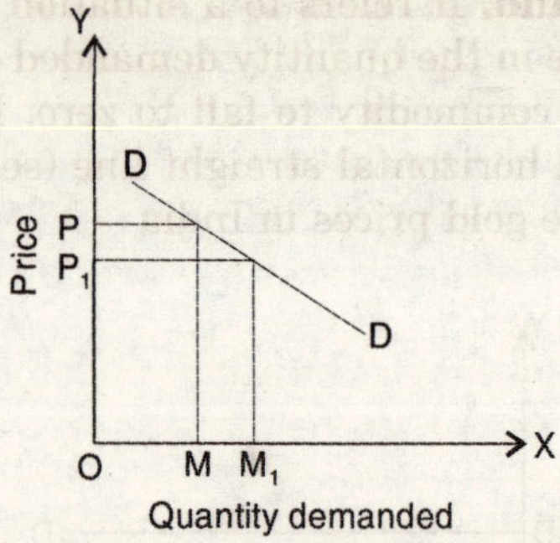

Fig. 3.8. Relatively elastic demand

4. **Relatively inelastic demand.** It is also known as elasticity of demand less than one (Pe < 1). It refers to a situation where a large change in price causes a small change in quantity demanded. Hence, it is called relatively inelasticity of demand or less than unity one. The demand curve is steeper in slope in this case (Pe < 1) refer Fig. 3.9

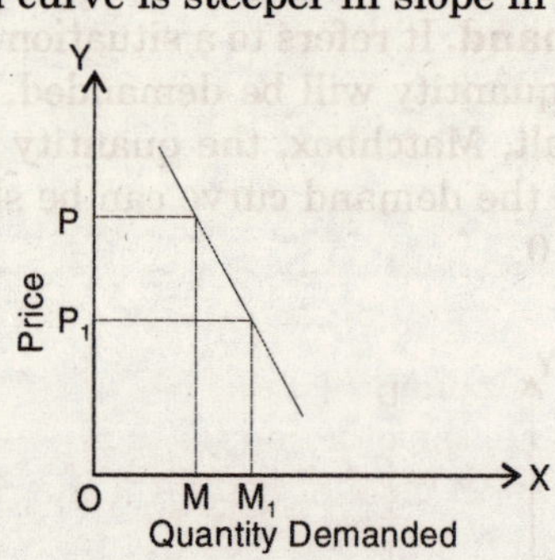

Fig. 3.9. Relatively inelastic demand

5. **Unitary elastic demand.** Unitary elastic demand is one where the proportionate change in quantity demand is exactly equal to the proportionate change in price. The demand curve slopes more or less uniformly. The change in price creates an equal change in the quantity demand. Hence, it is called unitary elastic demand. It is a rarity in the real world. Symbolically Pe = 1 (see Fig. 3.10)

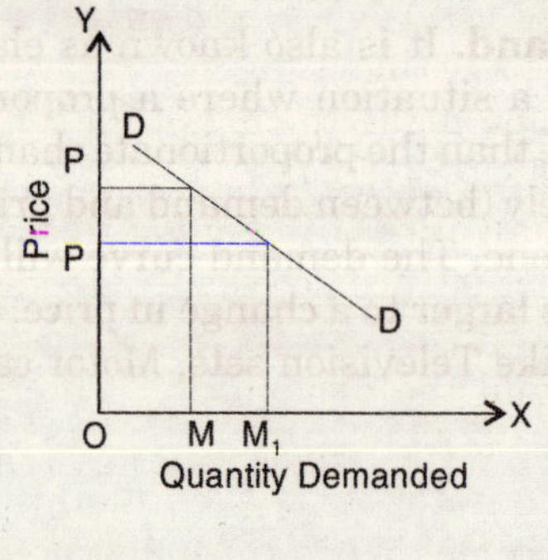

Fig. 3.10. Unitary elastic demand

FACTORS INFLUENCING PRICE ELASTICITY OF DEMAND

The term elasticity of demand refers to the responsiveness of a demand for a commodity or service to the changes in the variables confined to its demand function. According to professor **Marshall,** *"the elasticity or responsiveness in the market is great or small according as the amount demanded increases much or little for a given rise in price"*. The factors influencing the elasticity of demand are discussed below. The producer or the manager of a company must observe for conducive environment for his product to fit in and ascertain the factors for such an environment and device means to operate in the market.

Factors Influencing Price Elasticity
1. Nature of demand for the products
2. The number of uses of commodities
3. The level of income
4. The proposition of expenditure in the budget
5. The influence of habit
6. The level of prices
7. Substitute available for consumption
8. The degree of durability of goods

1. **The nature of demand for the product.** The elasticity of demand depends upon the nature and degree of commodities and luxuries. The demand for necessaries of life is ***inelastic***, for example, the demand for necessaries like food grains, salt, water, milk and the like. Whereas in case of comforts the demand is ***moderately elastic*** because with the rise or fall in the prices the demand for them decreases or increases moderately on the other hand, the demand for luxuries is ***elastic.*** Therefore a rise in price will result in reduction in demand and a fall in price leads to expansion of demand to a greater extent.
2. **The Number of uses of commodities.** Commodities having larger number of uses will have elastic demand and commodities having a few uses become inelastic demand such commodities are steel, coal, electricity and the like. Electricity is used for cooking, heating, lighting, and operating television and so on. If there is a small decrease in price of electricity its demand will increase to a greater extent, the demand may become elastic. If there is a rise in price then the electricity can be used only for very essential purposes and efforts will be made to curtail its consumption then the demand for electricity becomes inelastic.
3. **The level of income of an individual also determines elasticity of demand.** Generally, higher the level of income of an individual, his demand for commodity tends to be relatively inelastic because, the rich man does not bother about the changes in price. On the other hand the demand for commodities in case of lower income groups (LIG) tends to be relatively elastic.
4. **The proposition of income spent on consumption.** If the consumer spends a small proportion of his income on the consumption of commodities, the demand for that commodity will be inelastic. For example the consumer spends small expenditure of the budget on matchbox, salt, newspaper etc. But the commodities which entail a larger proportion of income on consumption, the demand for them is elastic. For example, items like food and clothing, the consumer spends a larger expenditure of his budget, hence the demand for these goods will be elastic.

5. **The influence of habit.** If consumers are addicted to the consumption of a particular commodity then the demand for that commodity will be inelastic. We may find that the price of coffee, cigarettes, liquor increases almost every year. But there has been a little effect on their demand because people are addicted to such habits.
6. **The level of prices.** The level of price also influences the elasticity of demand for commodities. There are some commodities like refrigerators, car, and interiors, which are highly priced in general. At a very high range of price the demand will be inelastic. However, if the price change is large at a very low range of price the demand will be inelastic.
7. **The substitute available for consumption.** If the commodities have close substitutes, the demand will tend to be elastic because with a rise in the price of one commodity, the demand for its substitute will immediately increase. For example, if the price of beverages such as Sprite, Thums Up, Coke, Maaza changes it will induce the people to substitute Limca, Goldspot, whose price remain constant. But in case of commodities that have no substitute like salt, potato, onion and the like the demand will be inelastic.
8. **The elasticity of demand also depends upon the degree of durability of goods.** In the case of durable goods like machinery, implements, the demand will be inelastic, whereas on the other hand the demand for perishable goods like fruits, vegetables, flowers the demand will be elastic. If the price of any of these goods changes the people may curtail or postpone their consumption.

Practical importance of Price Elasticity of Demand

Or

Some Business applications of Price Elasticity of Demand

The concept of price elasticity of demand has a practical significance in the formulation and understanding of economic policies and problems.

Practical importance of Price Elasticity
1. Public finance
2. Govt. economic policies
3. Exchange rate determination
4. Measuring the gains from international trade
5. Price determination under monopoly and imperfect competition
6. Determining rewards to factors of production
7. Determining joint product price
8. Shifting of tax burden

1. **Public finance.** This concept is very important to finance minister to formulate taxation and economic policies. In levying taxes on commodities the elasticity of demand for commodity should be taken in to consideration. To obtain adequate amount of revenue, he should impose more and more taxes on these commodities in which the demand is said to inelastic. On the other hand, if he impose more taxes on elastic goods the demand will contract and in turn it will reduce very much of total amount of revenue. That is why generally taxes are levied on commodities like kerosene, cigarette, matchbox and the like, the demand for these commodities are said to be inelastic.
2. **Government economic policies.** The elasticity of demand helps in framing economic policies and the knowledge of elasticity of demand is also very much required in fixing

the price of services rendered by public utilities such as water supply, electricity, posts and telegraphs and the like. The demand for these services is said to be inelastic and they are very essential in promoting the welfare of the people in the country. Suppose if these are left in the hands of private individuals, they will exploit the people by levying heavy taxes. Therefore the government should be able to provide essential goods and services to the public at reasonable rate by eliminating the monopolistic exploitation.

3. **Exchange rate determination.** Exchange rate refers to the rate at which the country's currency is exchanged for another country's currency. The elasticity of demand is very essential to determine the fixation of exchange rate between two currencies of two countries. To increase exports and to reduce imports the government of a country devalues its currency, which results in exports become cheaper and imports dearer, then the demand for Indian goods will increase in the international trade. Thus in deciding devaluation, the government should carefully consider the elasticity of demand for country's exports and imports in order to fix the exchange rate to correct disequilibrium in the balance of payments.
4. **Measuring the gain from international trade.** It refers to terms of trade and the rate at which the domestic commodity is exchanged for foreign commodity that will be determined by the relative elasticity of demand for the two countries. The domestic country will be benefitted from trade if she exports those goods in which the foreigners demand for Indian goods is inelastic (Indian cinema, Mysore silks, Jasmine, MTR products, and so forth) and imports those goods (capital goods) for which the demand is elastic.
5. **Determination of price under monopoly and imperfect competition.** The monopolist while fixing the prices for his/her commodity should carefully study the elasticity of demand for the product/service. If the demand for product is elastic, the monopolist will fix a lower price. On the other hand, if the demand for product is inelastic he will fix a higher price.

   In case of price discrimination, the monopolist will have rational price discrimination policy, that is he will charge different prices in different markets for the same product. In the market with less elasticity of demand for his product, he will fix a higher price and a market with more elasticity of demand for the product he will fix a lower price. Similarly, under imperfect competition there will be a large number of sellers, who will take into account the elasticity of demand for the product in fixing the price. If the demand for the product of a particular seller is elastic in relation to other sellers, he can attract new customers by lowering the price of his product. On the other hand, in case of inelastic demand he will fix a higher price.
6. **In the determination of rewards to various factors of production.** If the demand for industry's product is inelastic then the reward paid to various factors in the form of rent, wages, interest and profit will be greater and the case is reverse if the demand for industry's product is elastic.
7. **Determination of joint products price.** The elasticity of demand is very useful in the pricing of joint product such as wool and mutton, cotton and cottonseed. Among these products one can not ascertain the cost of production of each commodity and hence the price of each commodity is fixed on the basis of elasticity of demand. That is why the demand for commodities like wool, cotton, wheat and the like are inelastic and command a very high price and thereby products like mutton, cottonseed and straw have elastic demand.

8. Shifting of tax burden. It is possible for a businessman to shift a commodity tax or indirect tax in case of inelastic demand to his customers. But if the demand is elastic, he himself has to bear the tax burden. Otherwise demand for his goods will reduce.

MEASUREMENT OF PRICE ELASTICITY OF DEMAND

To know the extent of responsiveness or sensitiveness of demand for a commodity to the change in its own price, one can measure the price elasticity and can know the nature of elasticity of demand that is either more than one, less than one or unity. There are three methods that are available to measure the elasticity of demand. They are

(1) Arc method or mathematical method.

(2) Total outlay method and

(3) Point method.

This book focuses only on total outlay method for analysis.

Total Outlay Method

Outlay means expenditure for customer and revenue for seller. In the total outlay method, the elasticity of demand is calculated by taking into consideration the total outlay incurred on the purchase of commodity before and after a change in the price level.

Thus

Total outlay or total revenue = price × quantity (purchased or sold)

Prof. Marshall suggested that the easiest way of ascertaining whether or not demand is elastic is to examine the change in total outlay of the consumer corresponding to change in price.

There are three possibilities:

(i) With a fall in price or increase in price, if the total expenditure or total outlay remains the same, then the price elasticity of demand is equal to unity (one) or Pe = 1.

(ii) With the fall in price, if the total expenditure or total outlay increases, or with increase in price if the total expenditure decreases, then the price elasticity of demand is said to be less than unity (one) or Pe < 1.

(iii) With the fall in price, if the total expenditure or total outlay decreases, or with the increase in price, if the total expenditure increases, then the price elasticity of demand is said to be more than unity or (one) or Pe > 1.

Total outlay method of measuring the price elasticity of demand is portrayed in Table 3.4 for easy understanding.

Table 3.4: Total outlay method snapshot.

Situation	*Outlay*	*Nature of elasticity*
1	Total Outlay (TO) remains constant with the fall in price level (P)	Pe = 1
2	TO ↑ P ↑ TO ↓ P ↓	Pe < 1
3	TO ↑ P ↓ TO ↓ P ↑	Pe >1

The total outlay method can be explained in the form of a table (see Table 3.5).

Table 3.5

Illustration of Total outlay method of measuring price elasticity of demand

Price of a commodity	*Quantity demanded*	*Total outlay*	*Nature of price elasticity of demand*
Rs.	Units	Rs.	
5	100	500	Pe = 1
4	125	500	
5	100	500	
4	150	600	Pe = > 1
5	100	500	
4	120	480	Pe = < 1

The Measurement of elasticity of demand through total outlay method is explained in Fig. 3.11.

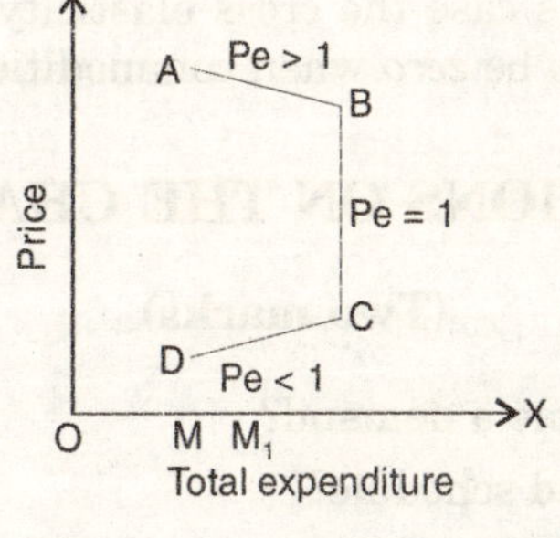

In the above figure the total outlay curve AB slopes downward indicating that, the total expenditure increases with a fall in price, then the price elasticity is more than one. BC the total outlay curve remains as a straight line indicating that the total expenditure remains constant with the fall in price, then the price elasticity is equal to one. CD is a total outlay curve which slopes downward from right to left indicating that with the fall in price the total outlay or expenditure decreases, then the price elasticity is less than one.

Income Elasticity of Demand

Income elasticity of demand refers to the rate of responsiveness of quantity demanded to a given change in income. It may be defined as "the responsiveness of a consumer's purchase of a particular good to a change in his income."

The income elasticity (Ey) can be measured by using the following formula:

$$Ey = \frac{\text{Proportionate change in quantities demanded}}{\text{Proportionate change in income}}$$

or

$$Ey = \frac{\text{Change in demand}}{\text{Change in income}}$$

CROSS ELASTICITY OF DEMAND

Cross elasticity of demand shows the relationship between the demand for two different commodities, *i.e.,* substitutes and complementary goods. Tea and Coffee are substitutes for each other, while car and petrol are complementary goods. The cross elasticity of demand may be defined as "*the proportionate change in the quantity demanded of a particular commodity in response to a change in price, not of the same commodity, but of another related commodity*".

The cross elasticity of demand (Ec) can be measured by using the following formula.

$$Ec = \frac{\text{Proportionate change in quantity demanded of 'X'}}{\text{Proportionate change in the price of 'Y'}}$$

Suppose commodities X and Y are substitutes then a rise in the price of 'Y' leads to an increase in demand for commodity 'X', Assume that the price of 'X' should remain constant. Thus the cross elasticity demand between substitutes goods is *positive.*

In case of complementary goods a rise in the price of one will lead to a fall in the quantity demanded for another good. In this case the cross elasticity of demand will be *negative*. The cross elasticity of demand is said to be *zero* when commodities are *independent* of each other.

QUESTIONS ON THE CHAPTER

(Two marks)

1. When does a desire become a demand?

2. What is meant by demand schedule?

3. What is meant by Individual demand?

4. Define market demand schedule.

5. What is meant by Demand Curve?

6. What is meant by Giffen's paradox?

7. What is Veblon's effect?

8. What is meant by exceptional demand curve?

9. What does the Elasticity of demand mean?

10. Mention three types of Elasticity of demand.

11. What do you mean by Price elasticity of demand?

12. What is Income elasticity of demand?

13. What does the Cross-elasticity mean?

14. Distinguish between change in demand and shift in demand.

15. Distinguish between extension of demand and increase in demand.

16. Mention the methods of measuring the price elasticity of demand.

17. What is meant by total outlay method?

(Five marks)

1. Explain why the demand curves always slope downward from left to right?
2. What is meant exceptional demand curve? Explain under what circumstances the Law of demand can not be applied.
3. Explain various types of price elasticity of demand?
4. Explain the total outlay method of measuring the Price elasticity of demand with a diagram.
5. Distinguish between Increase and Decrease in demand and Extension and Contraction of demand.

Essay Type Questions (Fifteen marks)

1. State and explain the Law of demand. What are its exceptions?
2. What does the Law of demand mean? Explain the factors that influence the demand for a product in a market.
3. What is the significance of demand analysis to a sales manager of a business firm? Explain the important determinants of demand.
4. What is meant by price elasticity of demand? Explain its business applications.
5. What is price elasticity of demand? Explain the total outlay method for the measurement of elasticity of demand. Mention the factors which influence elasticity of demand.

PROBLEMS ON TOTAL OUTLAY METHOD

Steps in solving the problems on measuring price elasticity of demand under total outlay method.

First step: Compute the total expenditure by multiplying price per unit (P) into quantity demanded (Q). (P × Q = Total expenditure)

Second step: Observe the Total expenditure column and arrive at the price elasticity by following the mentioned procedure:

(*i*) If the total expenditure increases with the fall in price, then the price elasticity of demand (Pe) is more than one. (Pe > 1).

(*ii*) If the total expenditure decreases with the fall in price, the Pe is less than one. (Pe < 1).

(*iii*) If the total expenditure remains same or constant with the fall in price, then the Pe is equal to one. (Pe = 1).

PRACTICAL PROBLEMS

1. (*a*) *What is demand forecasting?*

(*b*) *With the help of the following data, adopting 'Total Outlay Method" find out the price elasticity of demand and show the graphical representation.*

Situation	*Price per unit (in Rs)*	*Quantity demanded (in Units)*
(a)	*4*	*100*
	5	*90*
	2	*250*
(b)	*4*	*100*
	5	*80*
	2	*200*
(c)	*4*	*100*
	5	*70*
	2	*150*

Solution. Statement showing the computation of Price Elasticity of Demand

Situation	**Price per unit (in Rs.) (P)**	**Quantity demanded (in Units) (Q)**	**Total Outlay (P × Q = TE)**	**Nature of price elasticity of demand**
(*a*)	4	100	400	Pe > 1
	5	90	450	
	2	250	500	
(*b*)	4	100	400	Pe = 1
	5	80	400	
	2	200	400	
(*c*)	4	100	400	Pe < 1
	5	70	350	
	2	150	300	

The graphical representation of the price elasticity of demand is as follows (See Fig. 3.11).

2. *With the help of the following data, adopting total outlay method, find out the price elasticity of demand.*

Situation	*Price per unit (in Rs)*	*Quantity demanded (in Units)*
(a)	*12*	*500*
	10	*650*
	08	*900*
(b)	*12*	*500*
	10	*600*
	08	*750*
(c)	*12*	*500*
	10	*525*
	08	*625*

Solution.

Statement showing the computation of Price Elasticity of Demand

Situation	Price per unit (in Rs.) (P)	Quantity demanded (in Units) (Q)	Total Outlay (P × Q = TE)	Nature of price elasticity of demand
(*a*)	12	500	6000	Pe > 1
	10	650	6500	
	08	900	7200	
(*b*)	12	500	6000	Pe = 1
	10	600	6000	
	08	750	6000	
(*c*)	12	500	6000	Pe < 1
	10	525	5250	
	08	625	5000	

3. *With the help of the following data adopting total outlay method find out price elasticity of demand.*

Price per unit (in Rs.)	*Quantity demanded (in units)*
12	*5*
10	*8*
8	*12*
6	*15*
4	*18*
2	*20*

Solution.

Statement showing the computation of Price Elasticity of Demand

Price per unit (in Rs.) (P)	Quantity demanded (in Units) (Q)	Total Outlay (P × Q = TE)	Nature of price elasticity of demand
12	5	60 ↓	
10	8	80	Pe = > 1
8	12	96	
6	15	90 ↓	
4	18	72	Pe = < 1
2	20	40	

4. (*a*) *Explain briefly the Total Outlay method.*

(*b*) *With the help of the following data, adopting "Total Outlay method", find out the price elasticitiy of demand and show the graphical representation:*

Situation	*Price per unit (in Rs)*	*Quantity demanded (in Units)*
(*a*)	18.00	500
	16.00	650
	14.00	850
(*b*)	12.00	650
	10.00	750
	8.00	900
(*c*)	6.00	1200
	4.00	1800
	2.00	3600

Solution.

(*a*) Outlay means expenditure for customer and revenue for seller. Under the total outlay method, the elasticity of demand is calculated by taking into consideration the total outlay incurred on the purchase of commodity before and after a change in the price level.

Thus

Total outlay or total revenue = Price × Quantity (purchased or sold)

There are three possibilities:

(*i*) With a fall in price, if the total expenditure or total outlay remains the same, then the price elasticity of demand is equal to unity (one) or Pe = 1.

(*ii*) With the fall in price, if the total expenditure or total outlay increases, then the price elasticity of demand is said to be less than unity (one) or Pe = < 1.

(*iii*) With the fall in price, if the total expenditure or total outlay decreases, then the price elasticity of demand is said to be more than unity or (one) or Pe = >1.

(*b*) Statement showing the computation of price elasticity of demand by total outlay method

Situation	Price per unit (in Rs.) (P)	Quantity demanded (in Units) (Q)	Total Outlay (P × Q = TE)	Nature of price elasticity of demand
(*a*)	18.00	500	9000	Pe > 1
	16.00	650	10400	
	14.00	850	11900	
(*b*)	12.00	650	7800	Pe < 1
	10.00	750	7500	
	8.00	900	7200	
(*c*)	6.00	1200	7200	Pe = 1
	4.00	1800	7200	
	2.00	3600	7200	

For the graphical representation of the price elasticity of demand see Fig. 3. 11.

5. (*a*) *Explain the meaning of*

Ep > 1, Ep = 1 and Ep < 1

(*b*) *With the help of the data given below find out the nature of elasticity of demand (Use total outlay method).*

Situation	*Price per unit (in Rs)*	*Quantity demanded (in Units)*
(a)	*20* *15* *10*	*600* *900* *1400*
(b)	*20* *15* *10*	*600* *700* *800*
(c)	*20* *15* *10*	*600* *800* *1200*

Solution.

(*a*) Ep > 1, which means the price elasticity of demand is more than one.

Ep = 1, which means the price elasticity of demand is equal to one

Ep < 1, which means the price elasticity of demand is less than one.

(*b*)

Situation	**Price per unit (in Rs.) (P)**	**Quantity demanded (in Units) (Q)**	**Total Outlay (P × Q = TE)**	**Nature of price elasticity of demand**
(*a*)	18-00 16-00 14-00	500 650 850	9000 10400 11900	Pe > 1
(*b*)	12-00 10-00 8-00	650 750 900	7800 7500 7200	Pe < 1
(*c*)	6-00 4-00 2-00	1200 1800 3600	7200 7200 7200	Pe = 1

EXERCISE PROBLEM

1. Find out the nature of elasticity of demand from the following data by making use of total outlay method:

	Price per unit (in Rs)	*Quantity demanded (in Units)*
(*a*)	5.00 4.00	200 250
(*b*)	4.00 3.00	250 400
(*c*)	3.00 2.00	400 450

2. With the help of the following data, adopting total outlay method, find out the nature of price elasticity of demand.

	Price per unit (in Rs)	*Quantity demanded (in units)*
(*a*)	36 30 24	260 300 340
(*b*)	36 30 24	260 312 390
(*c*)	36 30 24	260 330 420

3. (*a*) State briefly the importance of price elasticity of demand.

(*b*) With the help of the table given below show different degrees of price elasticity of Demand.

Price per unit (in Rs.)	*Quantity demanded (in Units)*
9	5
8	15
7	20
6	30
5	36
4	45
3	55
2	70
1	90

4. (*a*) What is price elasticity of demand? State its different types.

(*b*) With the help of the following data, adopting total expenditure method, calculate the total outlay at each stage and find out price elasticity of demand.

	Price per unit (in Rs)	*Quantity demanded (in Units)*
(*a*)	20 15 10	300 450 700
(*b*)	20 15 10	300 350 400
(*c*)	20 15 10	300 400 600

SKILL DEVELOPMENT

1. When the sales of your product increase with the decrease in the price. Mention, which type of elasticity, is this?

2. List out from your everyday experiences the goods that have elastic demand and inelastic demand.

3. List a few examples for each exception to the law of demand from indian market scenario.

1. Giffen's Paradox
2. Veblon's Effect
3. False illusion or Psychological bias
4. Further increase in price (inflation)

4. Prepare an imaginary individual demand schedule and plot it on a diagram

5. Prepare an imaginary market demand schedule and construct a diagram.

6. List out some inferior and superior goods in the minds of indians.

7. Prepare a diagram showing increase and decrease in demand and extension and contraction of demand.

8. Construct a diagram showing measurement of price elasticity of demand on total outlay method.

CHAPTER

4

DEMAND FORECASTING

CHAPTER OUTLINE	LEARNING OBJECTIVES
— Nature of demand forecasting — Kinds or level of demand forecasting — Micro or firm level — Industry level — Macro level — Purpose or objectives of demand forecasting — Short-term — Long-term — Methods of demand forecasting — Survey methods — Opinion methods — Statistical methods	After reading this chapter, you should be able to : 1. Understand the meaning and definition of demand forecasting 2. Know different kinds or level of demand forecasting 3. Peruse the purpose or objectives of demand forecasting in the short and long run. 4. Diagnose the different methods of forecasting. 5. Workout problems on demand forecasting techniques.

A few number of companies in India who are manufacturing their products against order. But most of the companies produce their products in anticipation of demand. The success of these companies mainly depends upon the accuracy of predicting the demand for their products and also their closing inventory. This plays very important role in the cost structure of the product and profitability of the companies.

The success of a manufacturing organisation depends upon the good demand forecasting. The successful demand forecasting directly influences the functioning (activities) of various departments in an organisation. The purchasing of goods, production schedules, inventory plans, cash and capital expenditure budgets all depends upon the sales forecast. The success of sales forecasting of the large organisation depends on the established routine and top-level co-ordination. Hence usually in short-term demand forecasting, the companies will have a top level planning committee headed by a full-time planning manager comprising production, selling, and finance executives. For instance Bangalore Agenda Task Force (BATF) had some eminent industrialists, intellectuals, commissioners of departments like mahanagara palike, police, officers from BESCOM, BWSSB and BMTC for the planning and development of Bangalore.

Demand forecasting is one of the important activities of the management. The forecasting of demand helps to have optimum production programs, so that it is possible to avoid either over production or under production. It minimizes the total costs by avoiding over stocking of inventory during slack season, which reduces the risk of loss, obsolescence, capital block up, interest on capital invested, rent of the stores and the like.

The forecasting of demand or sales is not an easy task to a management. The demand for the product is influenced by various internal and external factors at micro and macro level. The demand forecasting should be accurate in the dynamic business world and because of **Globalisation Mantra** in almost all countries, there is a need for active demand forecast rather than passive demand forecasting.

The **Active Forecast** of sales refers to forecasting the demand for the product assuming that there will be change in the internal environment. For example like quality of a product, selling strategies, cost strategies and so on and external environment like government policies, competitors policies in pricing, economic situation of a country and so on.

The **Passive Forecasting** refers to forecasting the demand for the product assuming that there is change in the internal and external environment.

MEANING OF DEMAND FORECASTING

Demand Forecasting is an estimate of the demand for a product in future on the basis of statistical data based on past behavior and their relationship with the various determinants of demand.

Demand forecasting means an estimation of the level of demand that might be realised in future under given circumstances.

Kinds or Levels of Demand Forecasting

The demand forecasting may be undertaken at three different levels. They are at

1. Micro level or Firm level

2. Industry level and
3. Macro level

Micro Level or Firm Level Demand Forecasting

It refers to forecasting the demand for the product of a firm or at firm level. In this case the management of the firm is interested to forecast the demand for its product or products. For instance if the management of Hindustan Lever Limited forecasts the demand for its products like RIN detergent soap and Surf Excel it is micro level demand forecasting.

Industry Level Demand Forecasting

It refers to forecasting of demand for the product of an industry as a whole through its association of all the firms or through their trade unions. Industry refers to the aggregate of all the firms manufacturing same product or similar type of products as a substitute. For instance if KASSIA (Karnataka State Small Scale Industries Association) predicts the demand for the products of small scale industries with the entry of MNCs in the SS Industry in Karnataka, it is Industry level demand forecasting.

Macro Level Demand Forecasting

It refers to estimation of the demand for the goods at economy level or national level. For instance the Union Government in India predicts the demand for the agricultural products with the increase in population, change in the climate, change in the technology, import of goods from abroad and so on, this type of estimate of demand is macro level forecasting.

In addition to levels of sales forecasting of a product, the demand forecasting demands query for several aspects like

1. **Time factor.** It refers to questions like: Whether the demand forecasting is for long period or for the short period. The long period demand forecasting policy depends upon of the company, government, competition, and life cycle of the product and so on. Similarly the short period demand forecasting depends on its internal policies like sales promotion, tax laws and so on.
2. **Type of product.** Issues like whether the product is a new product or the product is already in the market, also influence the demand forecasting.
3. **Nature of a product.** The type of demand forecasting depends upon whether the product is capital goods and consumer durable or consumer goods.
4. **Factor to be studied.** The demand forecasting depends upon the factors to be studied like nature of competition, factors influencing the demand, factors influencing the purchasing behavior of customer, pricing method, promotional factors and so on and so forth.

PURPOSES OR OBJECTIVES OF DEMAND FORECASTING

The objectives of demand forecasting depend upon the outlook of an organisation. In general the business organisations will have long run objectives and short run objectives. They are:

Purposes of Long-run Forecasting

Long run is a period which is more than *one year, and this is up to five years.* In certain cases it is more than ten years. The purpose of this long-term demand forecasting is for very important factors.

Purposes of Long-run Demand Forecasting
1. Business planning
2. Financial planning
3. Manpower planning

1. **Business planning.** When a business unit is planning for long term huge investment, or, when it is planning for diversification of product, expansion of its existing capacity, or adding a new line of product, the business unit must forecast its demand for a long period. So that the company can recover its investment, survive in the market and also make profit in the long run.
2. **Financial planning.** When a business unit predicts the long-term demand for its product or products, naturally it has to think for long term financial planning to meet the requirement of long term demand for the product. It has to find out the financial requirements, plan for raising these resources, various long-term sources of funds, their rate of interest, and time and cost involved in raising of this finance.
3. **Manpower planning.** To meet the requirements of the long-term persistence demand for the product, the business unit must plan the manpower-requirement to manufacture the product forecast, if the products are labour oriented etc. The personnel department must forecast the required personnel for the manufacturing of the products predicted in the long run, and think it does it requires any training and development, to meet the growth of demand and so on and so forth.

Purposes of Short-term Demand Forecasting

Short term refers to the period that is less than one year. The business unit must forecast the demand for short-term, to meet the requirements of the market and to make them available in the market to maximise the profits.

Purposes of Short-term Demand Forecasting
1. Proper production policy
2. Suitable purchase policy
3. Suitable price policy
4. To fix sales targets
5. To fix short term financial plans.

1. **Proper production policy.** The success of production policy of a business unit also depends upon short-term demand forecasting. The business unit can produce adequate quantity of goods demanded only on proper demand forecasting. If there is no demand forecasting or if demand forecasting is not accurate then the business unit will produce either excess or deficit both of which are dangerous to an organisation.

2. **Suitable purchase policy.** The suitable purchase policy of an organisation depends upon proper demand forecasting in the short run. The purchasing department in an organisation can take required steps to purchase or replenish the stocks for stores on the basis of demand forecasting. So it will avoid excessive piling of stock or deficiency in the stock of goods for its manufacture. This will reduce the total cost of manufacture.
3. **Suitable price policy.** The price policy of an organisation depends upon the demand forecasting. If the organisation predicts that there is a heavy demand for the product in short run it can charge little higher prices. If the organisation predicts that there would be slackness in short run for the goods then it can charge reasonable price or give some discounts to encourage the sales.
4. **To fix sales targets.** The fixing of sales targets to the salesman of an organisation depends on short term demand forecasting. If a company predicts that there will be less demand for the goods in the short run, it can fix less sales target to the salesman so that they can achieve the targets and they will be motivated. If a company predicts that there is more demand for the goods in the short-run then it can fix higher targets, so that they can achieve and contribute to more sales.
5. **To fix short-term financial plans.** The short-term demand forecasting helps an organisation to formulate financial plans. The organisation can plan for providing necessary funds, devise means of acquiring such funds, and at what rate to raise funds etc, so that there may not be either excess of funds or deficit of funds.

Methods of Demand Forecasting

There is no common, easy and simple method to forecast the demand for the product of a firm. There are two ways of predicting demand for the product either by value judgments or using statistical techniques. These two are the extreme methods and hence a method that is blend of the two would be appropriate. The more commonly used methods of demand forecasting are:

I. Survey Methods

(*a*) *Consumer survey methods or direct interviews*

(*i*) Complete enumeration

(*ii*) Sample survey and

(*iii*) End-use method.

(*b*) *Opinion poll methods*

(*i*) Expert- Opinion method

(*ii*) Delphi method and

(*iii*) Market experimentation

II. Statistical Methods

(*a*) *Trend projection methods*

(*i*) Method of moving averages

(*ii*) Method of least squares

(*b*) *Regression analysis of econometric models*

(*a*) **Survey of buyers' intention or consumers survey.** Using the consumer survey method, a sample survey of the consumers may be undertaken by questioning (asking) them about their plan for purchase in the near future, their opinion about the commodity, about the price, the quality etc. In the consumer survey they can also ask the income of the potential group, whether they purchase with the marginal increase in price, through which media they knew about the product, and so on. A questionnaire may be prepared in this regard. This may be mailed to consumers or it may be sent through enumerators. This type of consumer's survey will provide excellent information on a number of important demand relationship such as price demand, income demand, advertisement demand, cross demand.

Merits of this method

1. This method is conducted to predict the short run demand.
2. This method is used when the number of consumers is large.
3. This method is suitable for industrial customers, whose number is usually less.

Drawbacks of this method

1. When the number of *consumers is very large,* this method is *expensive and time consuming.*
2. Consumers may *not show consistency and regularity* in buying intentions.
3. Consumers may *not be able to foresee the choice* when faced with many alternatives.
4. The plans of the consumer may *not be real but only wishful thinking.*

In the words of *Joel Dean* "a direct inquiry of customers has severe shortcomings in forecasting, in that industrial customers' plans may be trigger-sensitive to short-run economic changes, while consumers' plans are fragile, capricious, and expensive to collect".[1]

(*i*) **Complete enumeration method.** In this method all the potential consumers are contacted through questionnaire or schedule and they are asked about their future plan of purchasing the product. The addition of the quantities mentioned in the questionnaire gives the aggregate of the potential demand for the product from the customers. This method is applicable in the case of industrial goods whose number of customers is limited. This method is less costly when all the customers are located in nearby places, but because of the facility and edge provided by Internet, in this method more number of customers can be covered even though located at far off places.

This method suffers from the following limitations

✓ When consumers of the product themselves doesn't know the demand, then they may not answer questions.

✓ The answer under this method mostly becomes hypothetical (assumptive).

✓ The responses received may be biased because these answers are their own expectations

✓ The flexibility in the plans of production of the customers may bring big gap between the real demand and the expected demand for the product.

---

[1]Joel Dean, "Managerial Economics" , Prentice Hall of India Private Limited, New Delhi, p. 169.

(*ii*) **Sample survey method.** Under this method a sample of potential customers is selected from the market and served with a questionnaire or mailed questionnaire to sample customers. On the basis of the responses from the questionnaire and by adding the quantities mentioned in the questionnaire the probable demand for the product may be predicted.

Advantages of this method are

✓ It is simple and less costly

✓ It is less time consuming

✓ It is a more useful method in the case of business units for the market research

✓ This method works out like budget preparation in the government departments by collecting information from the budgeted expenditure from all the offices.

This method also suffers from the disadvantages of complete enumeration. Hence this method is also not fool proof.

(*iii*) **The end-use method.** The end use method of demand forecasting has a considerable theoretical and practical use, especially in case of forecasting demand for the inputs by the industrial sector. In this method the demand is forecast by obtaining information from the final users like industrial undertaking directly. In this method issues related to technological, structural and other changes which influence the demand are taken in to consideration while estimating the demand.

(*b*) **The collective opinion or opinion poll method.** Under this method, the opinion on the value judgment of the sales representatives, sales executives, marketing managers, business economist's and consultants is considered to predict the demand for the product. The opinion poll methods include:

(*i*) **Expert opinion method.** In this method the opinion of sales representatives about the probable demand for the product in their respective sales territories is collected. The aggregate of potential demand expressed by the sales representatives is arrived at this pool of opinion constitutes the total demand for the product.

This method is more appropriate in case of firms that have good network of sales representatives. These sales representatives will have close touch with the consumers or users of goods, so they can feel the pulse of the consumers and they can elucidate the real intentions of the consumers and probable demand for the product based on their experience. If there is no network of sales representatives then the company can take the opinion of professional market experts or consultants, to predict the demand for the product.

Merits

1. This method is simple and inexpensive and does not require any advanced statistical techniques.
2. The forecasts have the advantage of the first hand knowledge of the salesman.

Demerits

1. The Sales persons are biased observers because they may be pessimistic or optimistic.
2. Sales persons may not be aware of the macro economic changes in the economy, which may influence the demand. The sales representative's capacity to consider the macro economic changes like monetary policy, GNP, behaviour of the consumers may not be sound.

3. Sales persons may under estimate the demand which may for the company to set fewer sales target.
4. The estimates prepared by the sales representatives or professional experts are reliable only to the extent of their skill to analyze the market.
5. This demand estimates are subjective judgements of the assessors

(*ii*) **Delphi method.** It is an extension of the simple expert opinion poll method. In this method the divergent expert opinions of sales manager, economist, marketing manager, production managers are consolidated, then the compromise estimate of future demand for the product is arrived at through deliberations of these experts. It is a blind review technique to predict the future demand.

(*iii*) **The market experimentation.** It refers to a kind of controlled experiment in the market to study consumer behaviour in relation to the attempted changes in some demand determinants like price, advertisements, packing etc, by keeping other factors constant. This may help in finding the effects of changes in variables on the consumer demand. This method is often been conducted in the USA to gauge the effect of a change in some demand determinants like price, advertising, product design etc.

Demerits

1. This method is expensive and time consuming.
2. It involves risk because it may lead to unfavorable reactions from dealers, consumers and competitors.
3. It is also difficult to plan market experimentation under heterogeneous market conditions.

Statistical methods

The statistical methods utilise the historical data and cross-section data for estimating the demand for the product in the long run. The statistical methods are considered to be superior to the earlier methods because, under the statistical methods there is less scope for subjectivity and it is more scientific. The statistical methods are:

(*a*) Trend projection methods

(*i*) Method of moving averages

(*ii*) Method of least squares

(*b*) Regression analysis of econometric models

(*a*) Trend projection methods

Trend projection method refers to the projection of the sales of a product for the future on the basis of past demand. For this the statistical technique of time series is employed like moving average, method of least squares, regression analysis of econometric models and so on. It is a long term demand forecasting.

(*i*) **Method of moving averages.** Under this method of moving averages, the average value for a number of years is taken and this average is taken as the trend value for the future. While applying this method 3-yearly moving average, 5- yearly moving average, 8-yearly moving average and so on is selected. The period of moving average is to be decided in the light of the length of the cycle.

(*ii*) **Method of least squares.** Under this method, a trend line is fitted to the time-series sales data with the help of statistical techniques. The type of the trend equation that can be fitted to the time-series data is determined either by plotting the sales data or by trying different forms of trend equations for the best fit.

The most common type of trend equation is Linear Trend. When a time-series data reveals rising trend in sales, then a straight-line trend equation of the following form is fitted:

$$Y = a + bx$$

(*b*) **Regression analysis and econometric model building.** Most commonly, for demand forecasting purposes, the parameters of the demand function are estimated with regression analysis by an equation of a set of observed data. In this regard, the following economic indicators may be considered.

(*i*) Personal disposable Income towards demand for consumer products.

(*ii*) Agriculture or farm Income towards demand for agriculture equipments and fertilizers.

(*iii*) Construction contracts for demand towards building materials.

(*iv*) Automobile registry over a period towards demand for car spare parts, petrol etc.

The managerial economist collects such information, attempts to establish relationship between the demand for a product and the economic indicator with the help of the method of least squares and derives the regression equation. The linear relationship will be expressed by the equation

$$Y = a + bx$$

Y= the demand for the product

X = the economic indicator or parameter.

After the regression equation is derived, the value of Y can be estimated for any value of X.

Criteria of a Good Demand Forecasting Method

Criteria
1. Accuracy
2. Simplicity
3. Plausibility
4. Economy
5. Quickness
6. Flexibility

1. **Accuracy.** As for as possible the method of demand forecasting used should result in accurate results although from such forecasting accurate demand forecast is very difficult.
2. **Simplicity.** The method of demand forecasting used for predicting demand should be very simple to understand and implement so that the results will be accurate.
3. **Plausibility (Correct interpretation of the results).** The methods used to predict the demand for the product and their results should be projected or interpreted properly otherwise they give different results.

4. **Economy.** The methods used for the demand forecasting should not cost more for the organisation. If the cost is more compared to the quantum of benefit of the organisation then the firm may not derive profit.
5. **Quickness.** The method used should project the demand for the product on time. If the results are delayed then it will not serve the purpose.
6. **Flexibility.** The method used for demand forecasting should be flexible to implement under different circumstances and situations.

What are the methods of demand forecasting for new products?

Methods of demand forecasting for new products are quite different from the established products. The new products offered by the company or an economy must study the economic and competitive characteristic of the product offered and it requires intelligent projection of demand.

Joel Dean[1] suggested a number of possible approaches to the problem of forecasting demand for new products.

Demand Forecasting for New Products
1. Evolutionary approach
2. Substitute approach
3. Growth curve approach
4. Opinion-polling approach
5. Sales experience approach
6. Vicarious approach

1. **Evolutionary approach.** Project the demand for the new product as an outgrowth of an existing old product for example the demand of new products of Life Bouy like Life Bouy Plus, Life Bouy Gold and New life Buoy can be projected from the demand from an existing product - Life Bouy.
2. **Substitute approach.** Analyse the new product as a substitute for some existing product of service for example the demand for Solar energy, wind energy can be predicted from the demand of Hydro energy.
3. **Growth curve approach.** Estimate the rate of growth and the ultimate level of demand for the new product, on the basis of the pattern of growth of established product. For example the rate of growth of demand for fashionable products can be forecast on the basis of growth of female population and the growth of their related products.
4. **Opinion-polling approach.** Estimate the demand for a new product by making direct inquiries from the ultimate purchasers, either by the use of samples or on a full scale.
5. **Sales experience approach.** Offer the new product for sale in a sample market, like super bazaar. Exhibit the product sample in front of a super bazaar, Departmental store, Fab mall, Metro cash and Carry and study the opinion of the consumers or customers before offering the product on a commercial scale.

[1]Joel Dean, "Managerial Economics" , Prentice Hall of India Private Limited, New Delhi, p. 172.

6. Vicarious approach. Survey consumer's reactions to a new product indirectly through specialised dealers.

QUESTIONS ON THE CHAPTER

(Two marks)

1. What do you mean by Demand forecasting?
2. What do you mean by Active forecasting of sales?
3. What are the levels of Demand forecasting?
4. What do you mean by survey of buyer's intention?
5. What is "opinion survey" method of forecasting?
6. What is sample survey?
7. What is meant by market experimentation?
8. What is Delphi method?
9. What is evolutionary approach of demand forecasting?
10. What does the vicarious approach of demand forecasting mean?

(Five marks)

1. Explain the purposes of long-term demand forecasting.
2. Explain the objectives of short-term demand forecasting.
3. What are the methods of forecasting Demand for a new product? Explain.
4. Explain the various criteria of a good Demand forecasting.
5. What is demand forecasting? What is the significance of demand forecasting?
6. Explain briefly the total outlay method.
7. State briefly the significance of 'economic indicator' in demand forecasting.

Essay Type Questions (Fifteen marks)

1. Explain the different methods of Demand forecasting.
2. What is demand forecasting. Explain survey of buyer's intention method and collective opinion method with their merits and demerits.
3. What is demand forecasting? How many levels are there? Explain its various purposes.
4. What is demand forecasting? Discuss any three methods of demand forecasting.
5. What is demand forecasting? Explain the various approaches in the demand forecasting for a new product.

PROBLEMS ON DEMAND FORECASTING BY THE METHOD OF LEAST SQUARE

PRACTICAL PROBLEMS

1. *The following data represents the annual sales of a Mega Company:*

Year	*1999*	*2000*	*2001*	*2002*	*2003*
Sales (Rs. in lakhs)	*190*	*220*	*260*	*198*	*256*

(*a*) *Find the trend values for each of the five years by using the method of least squares.*

(*b*) *Estimate the annual sales for the year 2004 and 2005.*

Solution. Formula to find trend values by least square method is

$$Y = a + bx$$

where,

$$Y = \text{Year}$$

$$A = \frac{\Sigma y}{\Sigma N}$$

Σy = Total sales of the given years

ΣN = Total number of years given

$$b = \frac{\Sigma xy}{\Sigma x^2}$$

$$\Sigma xy = (x * y)$$

x = Deviation from middle year

$x^2 = (x * x)$

Year	*Sales (Rs. in lakhs)* *y*	*x* *(deviation from midd year 2001)*	x^2	*xy*	*Trend value (in lakhs)*
1999	190	– 2	4	– 380	202.8
2000	220	– 1	1	– 220	213.8
2001	260	0	0	0	224.8
2002	198	1	1	198	235.8
2003	256	2	4	512	246.8
	$\Sigma y = 1124$		$x^2 = 10$	$\Sigma xy = 110$ (+ 710) – 600 110	

Calculation of trend value by using least squares

Formulae

$$Y = a + bx$$

$$a = \frac{\Sigma y}{\Sigma N} = \frac{1124}{5} = \mathbf{224.8}$$

$$b = \frac{\Sigma xy}{\Sigma x^2} = \frac{110}{10} = 11$$

x = Deviation from middle year

Now let us substitute the values for the above formula $Y = a + bx$

$$Y = a + bx$$

For the year 1999 = 224.8 + 11(– 2)
= 224.8 + (– 22)
= Rs. 202.8 lakhs

For the year 2000 = 224.8 + 11(– 1)
= 224.8 + (– 11)
= Rs. 213.8 lakhs

For the year 2001 = 224.8 + 11(0)
= 224.8 + (0)
= Rs. 224.8 lakhs

For the year 2002 = 224.8 + 11(1)
= 224.8 + 11
= Rs. 235.8 lakhs

For the year 2003 = 224.8 + 11(2)
= 224.8 + 22
= Rs. 246.8 lakhs

Estimation of Sales

$$Y = a + bx$$

For the year 2004 = 224.8 + 11(3)
= 224.8 + 33
= Rs. 257.8 lakhs

For the year 2005 = 224.8 + 11(4)
= 224.8 + 44
= Rs. 268.8 lakhs

2. *From the data given below find the trend value for each of the year using method of least squares and estimate the annual sales for the year 2006.*

Year	*1999*	*2000*	*2001*	*2002*	*2003*
Sales (Rs. in lakhs)	*90*	*120*	*160*	*90*	*160*

Solution

Year	*Sales (Rs. in lakhs)* *y*	*x* *(deviation from midd year 2001)*	x^2	*xy*	*Trend value (in lakhs)*
1999	90	– 2	4	– 180	102
2000	120	– 1	1	– 120	113
2001	160	0	0	0	124
2002	90	1	1	90	135
2003	160	2	4	320	146
	$\Sigma y = 620$		$x^2 = 110$	$\Sigma xy = 110$ (+ 300) – 410 110	

Calculation of trend value by using least squares

Formulae

$$Y = a + bx$$

$$a = \frac{\Sigma y}{\Sigma N} = \frac{620}{5} = \mathbf{124}$$

$$b = \frac{\Sigma xy}{\Sigma x^2} = \frac{110}{10} = 11$$

x = Deviation from middle year

Now let us substitute the values for the above formula $Y = a + bx$

$$Y = a + bx$$

For the year 1999 = 124 + 11(– 2)
= 124 + (– 22)
– Rs. 102 lakhs

For the year 2000 = 124 + 11(– 1)
= 124 + (–11)
= Rs. 113 lakhs

For the year 2001 = 124 + 11(0)
= 124 + (0)
= Rs. 124 lakhs

Estimation of Sales

$$Y = a + bx$$

For the year 2006 = 124 + 11(5)
= 124 + 55 = Rs. 179 lakhs

Here x = deviation from middle year 2001 to 2006 is 5 years

For the year 2002 = 124 + 11(1)

= 124 + 11 = Rs. 135 lakhs

For the year 2003 = 1124+ 11(2)

= 124 + 22 = Rs. 146 lakhs

3. *From the data given below find the trend values for each year using the method of least squares and estimate the annual sales for the year 2000 and 2001.*

Year	*1994*	*1995*	*1996*	*1997*	*1998*
Sales (Rs. in 000's)	*60*	*80*	*70*	*90*	*100*

Solution

Year	*Sales (Rs. in lakhs)* y	*x (deviation from midd year 1996)*	x^2	*xy*	*Trend value (in 000's)*
1994	60	– 2	4	– 120	62
1995	80	– 1	1	– 80	71
1996	70	0	0	0	80
1997	90	1	1	90	89
1998	100	2	4	200	98
	$\Sigma y = 400$		$x^2 = 10$	$\Sigma xy = 90$ (+ 290) – 200 90	

Calculation of trend value by using least squares

Formulae

$$Y = a + bx$$

$$a = \frac{\Sigma y}{\Sigma N} = \frac{400}{5 \text{ years}} = \mathbf{80}$$

$$b = \frac{\Sigma xy}{\Sigma x^2} = \frac{90}{10} = 11$$

x = Deviation from middle year

Now let us substitute the values for the above formula Y = $a + bx$

Y = $a + bx$

For the year 1994 = 80 + 9(– 2)
= 80 + (– 18)
= Rs. 62,000

For the year 1995 = 80 + 9(– 1)
= 80 + (– 9)
= Rs. 71,000

For the year 1996 = 80 + 9(0)
= 80 + 0
= Rs. 80,000

For the year 1997 = 80 + 9(1)
= 80 + (9) = Rs. 89,000

For the year 1998 = 80 + 9(2)
= 80 + (18) = Rs. 98,000

Estimation of Annual Sales

For the year 2000 = 80 + 9(4)
= 80 + (36)
= Rs. 1,16,000

For the year 2001 = 80 + 9(5)
= 80 + (45)
= Rs. 1,25,000

4. *The following data show the sales of fertilizers in Karnataka.*

Year	*1998*	*1999*	*2000*	*2001*	*2002*	*2003*
Sales (Rs. in 000's)	*166*	*184*	*142*	*180*	*338*	*420*

Using the least square method estimate the sales for the year 2004.

Solution.

Year	*Sales (Rs. in lakhs)* y	x *(deviation from middle year 2000 and 2001)*	x^2	xy
1998	166	– 2.5	6.25	– 425
1999	184	– 1.5	2.25	– 276
2000	142	– 0.5	.25	– 71
2001	180	0.5	.25	90
2002	338	1.5	2.25	507
2003	420	2.5	6.25	1050
	Σy = 1430		x^2 = 17.5	Σxy = 885 (+ 1647) – 762 885

X = deviation from middle year is in between 2000 to 2001 *i.e.,* – 0.5 (half year) to the middle year and 0.5 (half year) after middle year.

Calculation of trend value by using least squares

Formulae

$$Y = a + bx$$

$$a = \frac{\Sigma y}{\Sigma N} = \frac{1430}{6 \text{ years}} = 238.33$$

$$b = \frac{\Sigma xy}{\Sigma x^2} = \frac{885}{17.5} = 50.57$$

x = Deviation from middle year is divided in to two half's *i.e.,* January to December is devided in to Jan. to June and July to December.

Now let us substitute the values for the above formula $Y = a + bx$

$$Y = a + bx$$

For the year 1998 = 238.33 + 50.57(– 2.5)

= 238.33 + (– 126.43)

= Rs. 111.9(000's)

For the year 1999 = 238.33 + 50.57(– 1.5)

= 238.33 + (– 75.85)

= Rs. 162.48 (000's)

For the year 2000 = 238.33 + 50.57(– 0.5)

= 238.33 + (– 25.28)

= Rs. 213.05 (000's)

For the year 2001 = 238.33 + 50.57(0.5)

= 238.33 + 25.28

= Rs. 263.61 (000's)

For the year 2002 = 238.33 + 50.57(1.5)

= 238.33 + 75.85

= Rs. 314.18 (000's)

For the year 2003 = 238.33 + 50.57(2.5)

= 238.33 + 126.43

= Rs. 364.73 (000's)

Estimation of sales for the year 2004

$Y = a + bx$

= Rs. 238.33 +50.57(3.5)

= Rs. 415.30 (000's)

Problems on Regression Analysis of Economic Indicators

1. *The following equation is used to predict the demand for passenger transport by BMTC in Bangalore:*

$$Y = -2.9 + 0.57\,X$$

In which Y is the daily demand for passenger transport (in lakhs) and X is the estimated population (in lakhs). What is the daily demand for passenger transport in Bangalore for the year 2006, when its population is expected to touch 35,00,000.

Solution. The equation used to predict the demand for passenger transport is

$$Y = -2.9 + 0.57\,X$$

Now let us substitute the values given in the problem

$$\begin{aligned} Y &= -2.9 + 0.57\,X \\ &= -2.9 + 0.57\,(35 \text{ lakhs}) \\ &= -2.9 + 19.97 \\ &= \textbf{17.05 lakhs passengers per day.} \end{aligned}$$

Ans. The daily demand for passenger transport in Bangalore by the year 2006 would be for 17.05 lakhs passengers per day.

2. *A refrigerator manufacturing company observes that there is a relationship between consumers Personal Income Index and the purchase of refrigerator by them. In order to predict the demand for refrigerators in a city the following equation was used:*

$$Y = 0.1 + 0.199\,X$$

Where Y = Sale of refrigerator in thousand units

X = Index of consumer's disposable income

Income is estimated to be Rs. 210 as on 31 March 2000. With the help of economic indicators, find out the demand for refrigerator in the city.

(Bangalore University B.Com April/May 2000)

Solution. The equation used to predict the demand for refrigerators is

$$Y = 0.1 + 0.199\,X$$

Now let us substitute the values given in the problem

$$\begin{aligned} Y &= 0.1 + 0.199\,X \\ &= 0.1 + 0.199(\text{Rs. } 210) \\ &= 0.1 + 41.79 \\ &= \textbf{42.79 thousand units.} \end{aligned}$$

Ans. The demand for refrigerators in the city when the Disposable Income Index is Rs. 210 is for 42.79 thousand.

3. *The electrical company observes that there is a relation between sales of electric fans and advertisement expenditure spent by them. In order to forecast the demand for electric fans the following equation was used:*

$$Y = 500 + 3\,x$$

where Y = Sales of electric fans

X = Advertisement expenditure

The advertisement expenditure to be Rs. 200 thousand as on 31, March 2006. With the help of economic indicators, find out the demand for electric fans of a company.

Solution. The equation used to predict the demand for electric fans is

$$Y = 500 + 3X$$

Now let us substitute the values given in the problem

$$Y = 500 + 3X$$
$$= 500 + 3(200)$$
$$= 500 + 600$$
$$= \mathbf{1100\ thousands.}$$

Ans. The demand for electric fans if the advertisement expenditure is Rs 200 thousand will be 1100 thousand.

EXERCISE PROBLEMS

1. From the data given below find out the trend values for each of the 7 years using the method of least squares and estimate the annual sales for the year 1999.

Year	1992	1993	1994	1995	1996	1997	1998
Sales	80	95	120	83	102	100	120

2. From the data given below, find the trend values for each year using the method of 'Least squares' and estimate the annual sales for the year 2004.

Year	1999	2000	2001	2002	2003
Sales (Rs. in lakhs)	140	160	170	160	190

3. From the following data given below find the trend values for each year using the method of least squares and estimate the annual sales for the year 2006

Year	1999	2000	2001	2002	2003	2004
Sales (Rs. in lakhs)	*20*	*36*	*50*	*64*	*60*	*70*

4. Export sales of a company for the last 5 years are:

Year	1999	2000	2001	2002	2003
Sales (Rs. in lakhs)	50	62	88	68	80

Project trend of exports sales for the next four years

SKIL DEVELOPMENT

1. Conduct a survey in your locality to launch a product of any one of the new FMCGs.

2. Conduct a survey of 30 families residing in different localities with different income groups to find out the products they buy (for daily and occasional use). Group these products on the basis of their income groups and analyse or observe the relationships.

(*a*) Products: Toilet soaps, Tooth paste, Hair oil, Face powder, Creams, Wheat flour, Quality of rice, Edible oil, etc.,

(*b*) Sex: Men/Women

(*c*) Monthly income

3. Identify different models adopted by various companies to forecast new products.

CHAPTER

5

LAW OF SUPPLY

CHAPTER OUTLINE	LEARNING OBJECTIVES
Supply — Law of supply — Difference between supply and stock — Determinants of supply — Exceptions to law of supply — Production function (input-output analysis) — ISO-quant and ISO-cost curves — Managerial uses of production function — Law of variable proportions — Incraesing, constant and diminishing returns — Economies of scale — Meaning — Internal and external economies — Diseconomies of large scale production	After reading this chapter, you should be able to : 1. Know the law of supply 2. Differentiate between supply and stock 3. Analyse the determinants of supply 4. Identify the exceptions to the law of supply 5. Understand production function 6. Differentiate between ISO-quant and ISO-cost curves 7. Know the managerial uses of production fucntion 8. Understand the law of variable proportions 9. Distinguish between increasing, constant and diminishing returns 10. Know the economies of scale and its kinds 11. Identify the diseconomies of scale

In economics, supply during a given period of time means the quantities of goods offered, for sale at particular prices. Thus, the supply of a commodity may be defined as *the amount of that commodity which the sellers or producers are able and willing to offer for sale at a particular price during a certain period of time.* Supply is a relative term. It is always studied with reference to price and time.

Difference between Supply and Stock

The following are the differences:

1. Supply is a part of stock offered for sale at a given price. Where as the stock refers to total goods possessed by the seller. For instance if a whole sale dealer of wheat has 20 tons of wheat in the godown, but he does not offer entire wheat for sale on a particular day, it is called stock possessed by him. If he offers for sale only *one ton* out of 20 tons on that day when the price is reasonable to him, it is called supply.
2. Stock is a potential supply (20 tons), where as supply is an Actual supply (one ton).
3. Stock may exceed supply but supply cannot exceed stock.

DETERMINANTS OF SUPPLY

The following are the determinants of supply.

Determinants of Supply
1. Price
2. Cost of factors of production
3. The state of technology
4. Factors outside the economic sphere
5. Tax and subsidy
6. The goals of firms

1. **Price.** One important factor that determines the supply of a product is price. When the price of a commodity is more then the supply of a commodity will also be more or vice verse.
2. **The cost of factors of production.** The supply is reduced when the cost of factors of production increases. The price of the factors of production increases, the cost of production also would increases.
3. **The state of technology.** Improved technology results in large-scale production and lower cost of production, which leads to increase in supply.
4. **Factors outside the economic sphere.** Weather conditions, floods and draughts, epidemics, war etc, also would cause fluctuation in the supply of goods.
5. **Tax and subsidy.** If tax is imposed on a commodity or a factor of production it raises the cost of production, consequently, the production is reduced due to less demand. A subsidy is another factor which provides incentive to production and to increase the supply.
6. **The supply of a commodity depends upon the goals of firms.** Supply of a commodity increase if the producers desire to sell as much as possible, even at the cost of profits. Supply is reduced if the producers desire to derive maximum profits.

LAW OF SUPPLY

There is a direct relationship between price and supply. Price is an independent variable and Supply is dependent variable. The supply of goods to the market varies directly on its price in the markets. More is supplied at higher price and less at lower price. This law is explained with the help of table and diagram (on Table 5.1 and Fig. 5.1).

Tabular Representation of Law of Supply

Table 5.1. Law of supply

Price per unit (in Rs.)	Supply (in units)
5	50
10	100
15	150
20	200
25	250

If the information contained in the table is depicted on the OX and OY axis, what is observed is an upward sloping supply curve indicating that more will be supplied at higher prices and less will be supplied at lower prices.

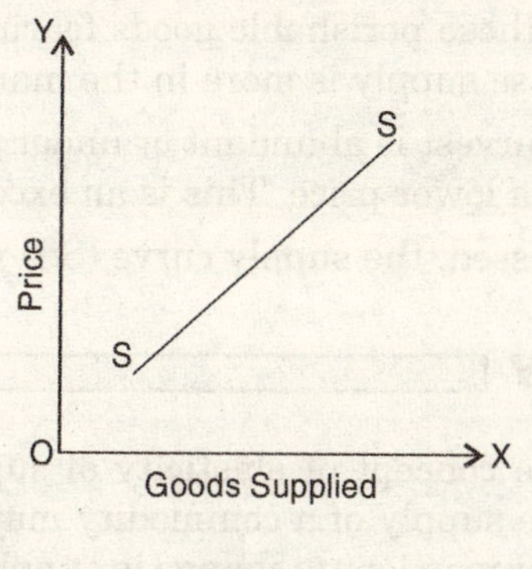

Fig. 5.1

The goods supplied to the market is plotted on OX axis and on OY axis, the price of the good is represented. At Rs. 5 per unit 50 units are supplied, at 15 rupees price, 150 units are supplied, whereas 250 units are supplied at Rs. 25 per unit. Thus, obviously the supply curve (SS) slopes upward.

EXCEPTIONS TO LAW OF SUPPLY

Usually there is a direct relationship between variables, price and supply. But under certain circumstances even though the price rises, supply will be less and at times, price decreases but supplies increases. These peculiar situations are called exceptions to the Law of Supply. The following are the exceptions to the Law of Supply.

Exceptions to Law of Supply
1. Increase in income
2. During the war
3. During the national calamities
4. High unemployment rate
5. Perishable goods
6. Good harvest

1. **Increase in income.** Whenever the income of the people increases some self contended employees will not work further extra hours or assume extra paid work. For example after implementation of UGC scales to teachers, many of them declined to take evaluation work. In fact they seem to desire to more leisure time to spend along with their family on holidays/vacation. This is a good example of exception to Law of Supply.
2. **During the war.** Even in war times, people won't come for work at the cost of their lives, even at higher wages. This is another exception to the law.
3. **During the national calamities.** People will decline to accept the job after or during the earthquake, tremor, flood and other natural calamities.
4. **High unemployment rate.** Even though the labour rate is less in under developed and developing countries like India, where unemployment rate is more, people work for less price, that means supply of labour is more whatever may be the labour rate.
5. **Perishable goods.** If the demand is less for perishable goods, price will be low and the traders will supply these perishable goods fearing perishability of goods further at lower price, in this case supply is more in the market at reduced price.
6. **Good harvest.** When harvest is abundant or under good yield the supply of goods in the market would be at a lower price. This is an exception to the Law of Supply.

In the circumstances discussed, the supply curve (SS) will slope downwards.

ELASTICITY OF SUPPLY

Like elasticity demand, the concept of elasticity of supply tells the responsiveness of supply to the change in price. The supply of a commodity may be elastic or inelastic. A small change in price causes more than proportionate change in supply which is called **elastic supply.** A small change in price leads to less than proportionate change in quantity supplied which is called **inelastic supply.**

The formulae used to measure the elasticity of supply are:

$$Es = \frac{\text{Proportionate change in quantity supplied}}{\text{Proportionate change in price}}$$

Symbolically it is represented as follows

$$Es = \frac{\Delta q}{Q} / \frac{\Delta p}{P}$$

or

$$Es = \frac{\Delta q}{q} \times \frac{p}{\Delta p}$$

For example if the price of a commodity X increases from Rs 3,000 per unit to Rs. 3,500 per unit, consequently the quantity supplied increases from 4,000 units to 5,000 units. Then the elasticity of supply will be as follows:

$$Es = \frac{\Delta q}{Q} \times \frac{\Delta p}{P}$$

$$Es = \frac{1000}{4000} \times \frac{3000}{500} = \mathbf{1.25}$$

CONTRACTION AND EXPANSION OF SUPPLY AND INCREASE AND DECREASE IN SUPPLY

There is distinction between contraction and expansion of supply and increase and decrease in supply like in the case of demand. Expansion and contraction of supply is due to change in prices of a commodity.

Expansion of supply refers to, other things remaining equal, if the supply of a commodity will expands (increase) if there is a rise in price.

Contraction of supply refers to, other things remaining equal, if the supply of a commodity contract (decrease) there is a fall in price. In the case of expansion and contraction of supply the movement is along the supply curve as shown below in the supply curve SS with arrow marks.

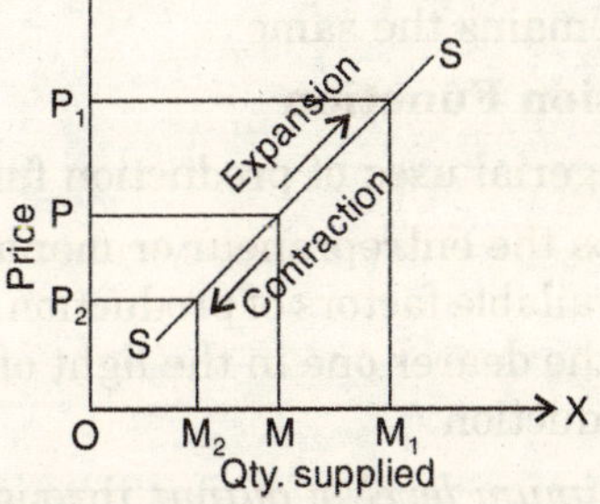

Fig. 5.2.

Increase and decrease in supply is due to change in various other factors of supply like change in technology, good economic conditions, state encouragement etc., other than price. **Increase in supply** refers to, large supply of a commodity at the old price or the old quantity at a lower price.

Decrease in supply refers to, smaller quantity of supply at the old price or the old quantity of supply at a higher price.

The increase and decrease in supply is represented on a graph in the figure below. The increase in supply is shown below the actual supply curve SS, which is represented as $S^1 S^1$. The decrease in supply is represented as S^2, which lies above the actual supply curve SS.

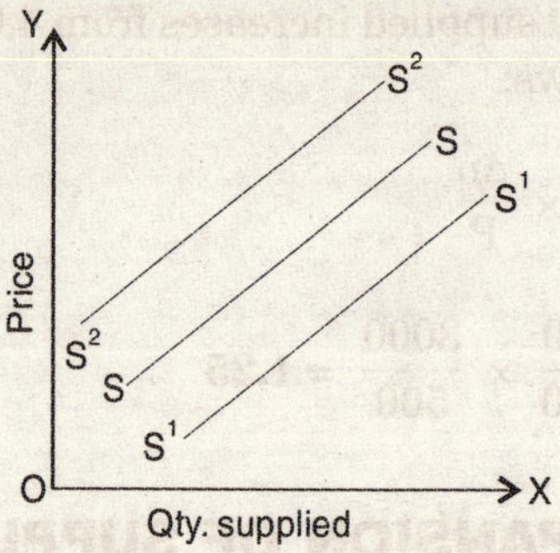

Fig. 5.3

Production function

Production refers to conversion of inputs (resources) into output (Finished commodity). In the production process, a firm combines various inputs in different quantities and proportions to procure different levels of outputs. Indeed, the rate of output of a commodity functionally depends on the quantity of inputs used per unit of time. This technological, physical relationship between inputs and outputs is called production function.

Definition. A production function refers to the functional relationship between physical levels of input and output of a firm, per unit of time under the given technology.

In algebraic terms, the production function may be put as.

$$Q = f(a, b, c, d \ldots\ldots n\, T) \quad \text{in a prevailed technology.}$$

Where as T = Technology remains the same

Managerial use of the Production Function

The following are the managerial uses of production function.

1. Production function helps the entrepreneur or manager to *determine least cost factor combination* out of the available factors of production. The businessman can substitute cheaper factors against the dearer one in the light of the production function and can minimize the cost of production.
2. It helps *to determine optimum level of output* through production equilibrium.
3. It serves as the basis of *programming technique* in production planning.
4. It is useful in *making important decisions about cost economy and equilibrium level of output.*

Production Function with two Variable Inputs

Iso-quants

It is also called product Curve Equal product curve put production indifference curve. The concept of production iso-quant is similar to the concept of indifference curve. The Iso-quant curves represent the various combinations of two variable input produces at the same level of output. The Table 5.2 shows the various combinations of labour and capital result in the same output.

Table 5.2

Combination of two factors of production produces same quantity or output

Units of labour	Units of capital	Total output (units)
1	10	10
2	8	10
3	6	10
4	4	10
5	2	10

The above table clearly explains that 10 units of output can be produced with 1 unit of labour and 10 units of capital or 2 units of labour and 8 units of capital or any other combination shown in the table. The same figures are plotted on a diagram to draw a Iso-quant curve.

Diagrammatic representation of Iso-quant curve:

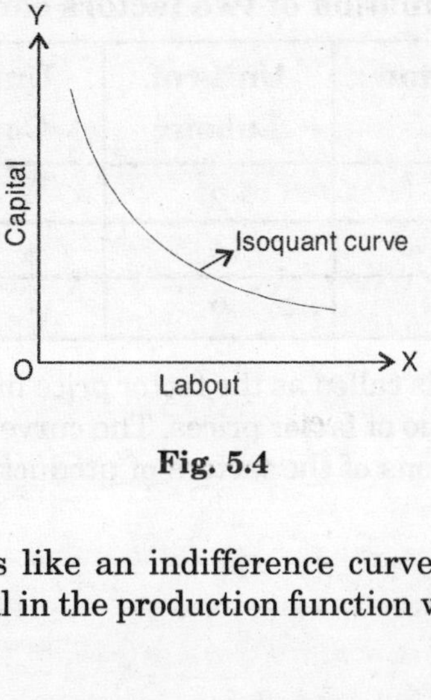

Fig. 5.4

The Iso-quant curve looks like an indifference curve, which shows that the various combinations of labour and capital in the production function will produce same quantity (10) of output.

PROPERTIES OF ISO-QUANT

The following are the important properties or characteristics of iso-quants.

1. **Iso-quants have a negative slope.** The Iso-quant curve slopes downward from left to right. This is because, when the amount of one factor input is increased that of the other must be decreased. At each point on the Iso-quant curve one gets factor combination which produces the same level of output.
2. **Iso-quant are convex to origin.** This is because of the marginal rate of technical substitution. According to the marginal rate of technical substitution, the rate of reduction in one factor increases an additional unit of another factor in the combination.
3. **Iso-quants do not intersect.** The iso-quants do not intersect because each iso-quant represents a different quantum of output. Therefore, if two iso-quants intersect each

other it would involve logical contradiction that there is similar level of quantity of production from two factors of production at different combinations.

4. **The iso-quant curve is an oval shaped curve.** It must be noted that the iso-quant curve may have positive upward slope at its ends. This is because when a relatively small amount of a factor is combined with a relatively large amount of another factor, in such a manner that the marginal productivity of this abundant factor tends to be negative and as such resulting in a decline in the total output.
5. **A higher iso-quant represents larger output.** The higher iso-quant curve represents larger output is produced with the same quantity of one input and larger quantity of the other input.

Iso-Cost Curve or Factors Price Line:

Assuming that a firm has Rs. 100 to spend on capital and labour in the production function, further it is assumed that the prices of factors remains constant and are divisible. If the price of capital is Rs. 20 per unit and the price of labour is Rs. 10 per unit, Firm can buy either 5 units of capital or 10 units of labour or any other combination with the help of Rs 100 shown in the Table 5.3

Table 5.3. Combination of two factors can be purchased

Combination	Units of Labour	Units of Capital
A	2	4
B	4	3
C	6	2

In the diagram the line CD is called as the factor price line as it indicate the factor prices. The slope of the line shows the ratio of factor prices. The curve is also called as the Iso-cost line as it shows the various combinations of the factors of production, which can be bought with a given cost or money or finance.

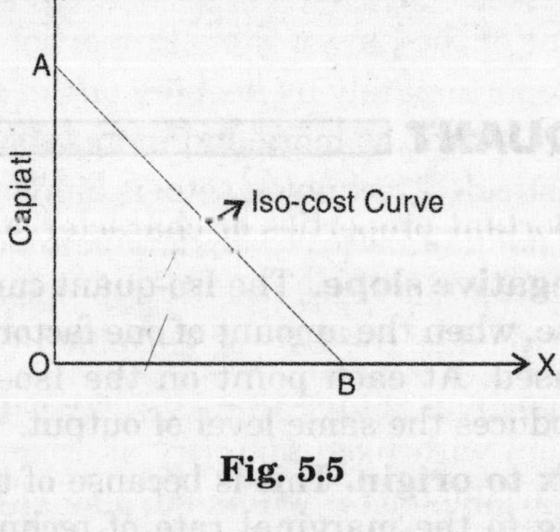

Fig. 5.5

Equilibrium Through Iso-quant and Iso-cost Curve
Or
The Least Cost Combination of the Factors of Production

To explain the equilibrium through Iso-quant and Iso-cost curve, let us take the production indifference map of iso-quant curves. *Production Iso-quant Map* refers to a set of Iso-quant curves. Each Iso-quant curve represents different levels of output from different combinations of factors of production. In the diagram we have the factor price (Iso-cost) line CD and iso-quants indicating the output levels of 10,20,30 etc. The firm reaches the equilibrium at point 'K' *i.e.,* the point of tangency between the iso-cost curve and the iso-quant curve representing the output of 20 units. Firm employs OI units of capital and OL units of labour in order to produce 20 units of output. The firm will not choose the iso-quant representing the output 10 as it is below the iso-cost curve and it is beneficial to the firm to reach a higher iso-quant. The firm is unable to reach the Iso-quant of 30 units as it is above the reach of the firm. The optimum combination is represented by the tangency between the iso-quant and the factor price line.

The diagrammatic representation of optimum combination or equilibrium through iso-quant and iso-cost curves is shown below in Fig. 5.6.

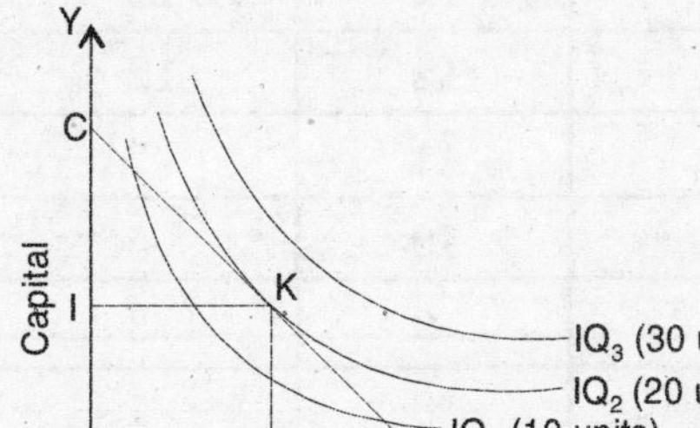

Fig. 5.6

LAW OF VARIABLE PROPORTIONS

The law of variable proportions is the fundamental law of production. This is also known as the Law of Diminishing Returns or the Law of Non - Proportional Returns. This law operates when some factors are varied proportionately by keeping one of the factors constant. It is the practical experience of every farmer that as more and more labour and capital (in the form of fertilizer, high yielding seeds, pesticides, technology etc) is employed on the same piece of land, the total returns increase, after a point, it increases less than proportionately or at a diminishing rate. This tendency of total product to increase less than proportionately is called the Law of Diminishing Returns. It is also called as the Law of Variable Proportions.

The Law of Variable Proportions states that, if increasing quantities of one factor of production are used in conjunction with fixed quantity of other factors, then, after a certain point, each successive unit of a variable factor will make a smaller and smaller addition to the total product.

According to **Albert L. Meyers** *"If one or more factors of proportion are held constant and one or more factors are allowed to vary in amount, the total output will not vary in continuous proportion to the amount of variable factor employed".*

John M. Cassels, states that "*in a given state of the arts, after a certain point is reached, the application of further units of any variable factor to another fixed factor (or fixed combinations of factors) will yield less than proportionate returns.*"

Illustration. Let us assume that a farmer has 5 acres of cultivable land that remains constant. Assume further that he wants to increase the output of this farm. In order to do this he has to increase the employment of labour and capital. The different units of labour and capital employed are shown in the Table 5.4.

Table 5.4

The TP, AP and MP at various units of labour and capital employed

Units of L + C	Total product	Average product	Marginal product	
1	8	8	8	
2	20	10	12	
3	36	12	16	
4	48	12	12	I Phase
5	55	11	7	
6	60	10	5	
7	63	9	3	
8	64	8	1	II Phase
9	64	7.1	0	
10	60	6	– 4	III Phase

In the example, it is clear that as the farmer goes on increasing the application of labour and capital on the same plot of land, in the beginning the total product increases more than proportionately and after a point it shows a tendency to increase but at a diminishing rate.

Diagrammatic representation of the law

Diagramatic representation

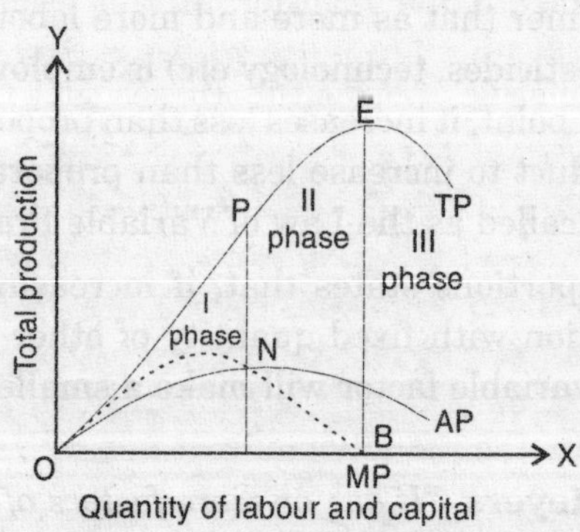

The operation of the law exists in three stages.

In the first phase, the total product increases along with an average product per unit of variable factor. The total product increases more than proportionately. The phase ends at a point where average product is equal to marginal product.

In the second phase, the average product per unit of variable factor decreases and the total product increase less than proportionately. This phase comes to an end at a point where the total product is highest and marginal product is zero. Total product still increase during this phase.

In the third phase of the law, T.P decreases, A.P continues to decrease and M.P becomes negative.

Only stage II is rational to the producer side. It is a relevant range for a rational firm to operate. No firm will choose to operate either in stage I or stage III. In stage I, it is profitable for the firm to keep on increasing the use of labour and in stage III M.P is negative and hence it is inadvisable to use additional labour. The firm therefore, has a strong incentive to expand through stage I into stage II.

Assumptions of this Law

This law is based on the following assumptions.

1. **Constant technology.** This law assumes that the technology remains constant because the change in technology will have its impact on the productivity. The use of sophisticated technology changes the marginal and average product. The marginal and average product may rise instead of diminishing.
2. **Short run.** The law operates in short run because only in the short run, one of the factors is fixed and others are variable. In the long run all factors are variable.
3. **Homogeneous input.** The variable input, which is applied unit by unit, is homogeneous in amount and quality.
4. It is possible to use various amounts of variable factors on the fixed factors of production.

ECONOMIES OF LARGE SCALE PRODUCTION

The scale or size of production will determine the cost of production. If the scale of production is small, then the cost of production will be high. If the scale of production of a firm is large, obviously the cost of production will be less. This is due to economies of large-scale production. The economies of scale are due to either internal economies or external economies. *Economies of scale* in a broad sense is anything which serves to minimize average cost of production in the long run as the scale of output increases that is refereed to as 'economies of scale'.

Classification of economies of scale. The economies of scale is classified into internal economies and external economies.

Internal Economies are those economies, which are open to an individual firm when its size expands. These are solely enjoyable by the firm itself when its scale of production increases, independent of the actions of others firms. For instance if the production of a firm increases the firm is benefitted by the reduction of cost due to bulk purchase of raw material, more application of labour and specialization of labour, easy availability of finance, increased working capital and its expansion and so on.

External economies are those economies which are shared by all the firms in an industry or in a group of industries when their size expands. They are available to all firms from outside, irrespective of their size and scale of production. They are the result of the growth and expansion of any particular industry or a group of industries as a whole.

Distinction between Firm and Industry

A firm refers to a single productive unit *e.g.* an individual unit producing sugar is a firm or Raymond's is a textile firm. Industry refers to a group of firms producing the same commodity or product *e.g.* all firms producing sugar in a country constitute the sugar Industry or all firms manufacturing textiles in a country constitute the Textile Industry.

Forms of Internal Economies

The internal economies are of various forms they are.

Forms of internal economies

1. Labour economies
2. Technical economies
   (*a*) Economies of superior techniques
   (*b*) Economies of increased dimensions
   (*c*) Economies of linked process
   (*d*) Economies of power
   (*e*) Economies of by-products
   (*f*) Economies of continuation
3. Managerial economies
4. Marketing economies
5. Financial economies
6. Risk bearing economies
   (*a*) by diversification of output
   (*b*) by diversification of market
   (*c*) by diversification of sources of supply.

1. **Labour economies.** With the increased production the labour force in the organisation increases, which may further lead to division of labour and greater degree of specialisation. Moreover a large firm attracts more efficient labour by mobility of factors and also through promotion. All this increases the specialisation in the production process, which ultimately reduces the cost of production.
2. **Technical economies.** Technical economies are those economies which reduce the cost of manufacturing process itself. The technical economies are:

   (*a*) ***Economies of superior technique.*** The economies of superior techniques are available to a firm when it expands its production by installing superior techniques of production so that the cost of production decreases. The firm using old and outdated techniques of production can not produce at lesser cost. For instance in the cellular phones market with the introduction of superior techniques the features in product are improvised and the price of the phone gets reduced substantially.

(b) ***Economies of increased dimension.*** This type of economy is available to a firm when it expands its dimension. It is purely a mechanical advantage of using large machines. For example by increasing dimension of the truck from two-ton capacity to nine-ton capacity or to 30-ton capacity the cost of carrying per ton will decrease. For instance the manufacturing of VOLVO trucks by the Swedish company, the revolution in the capacity of carrying the goods has been introduced in the transport industry and reduction in the cost of transportation is achieved.

(c) ***Economies of linked process.*** When the process of production is properly linked in a continuous sequence the loss in time can be saved and the wastage in the process can be reduced.

(c) ***Economies of power.*** When large machines are installed in large firms, the consumption of power in the process can be achieved when compared to the machines used in the small firms.

(e) ***Economies of by-products.*** The large firms can make use of the raw materials more economically by producing by-products out of the waste in the process. This ultimately reduces the cost of manufacturing. For instance while producing sugar, the wastes like molasses and cane pulp can be used in liquor industries and paper industry respectively which reduces the cost of production of the main product (sugar). The recent decision to mix ethenol (a by product from molasses) with petrol will further reduce the cost of sugar.

(f) ***Economies of continuation.*** If a company produces products continuously in large scale the technical cost of manufacturing will reduce. For example the cost of printing for 1,000 copies of invitation would be Rs. 5 per invitation. But for a bulk order of 10,000 copies the rate could be as low as Rs. 2.

3. **Managerial economies.** Managerial economies arises because of specialization of labour and mechanization of managerial functions. If the production is made in large scale the same managerial personnel can handle the production process efficiently, so the cost of production will reduce.
4. **Marketing economies.** Marketing economies are economies of buying and selling. A large firm can generally buy more cheaply than a small firm can. It can also achieve economy of transportation. Similarly the large firms will enjoy market preferences. Only single advertisement of a big organisation will promote their entire line of products.
5. **Financial economies.** Large firms will have greater advantages than the smaller one in financial matters. These organisations can raise funds easily in the internal market and abroad through FDIs, FIIs, ADRs, GDRs and so on because the investors will come forward to invest their funds in large firms than in the small ones. In addition to this the large firms can issue their shares at premium.
6. **Risk- bearing economies:** Large firms can minimize or eliminate business risks by producing wide range of products. These firms can spread risks in the following ways.

   I. ***By Diversification of output.*** A big firm can produce a number of product lines. Loss in one product can be compensated with the profits of other products. For example if loss arising from one of the products of HLL (Nirma detergent) is compensated from the other products like soaps, talcum powder and so on.

   II. ***By diversification of market.*** When the product is manufactured in large scale and sold in various markets in different states throughout the country, the loss in one state or area can be compensated from the market in other markets or areas.

III. ***By diversification of sources of supply as well as of process of manufacturing.*** In the large organisation the shortage of raw materials, power, capital is comparatively less because they will procure from other alternative sources.

Forms of External Economies. The forms of external economies are

Forms of External Economies
1. Economies of localisation
2. Information of technical and market intelligence
3. Economies of vertical disintegration
4. Economies of by products

1. ***Economies of localisation.*** The growth of an industry increases the concentration of firms in the same area by which they derive mutual advantages through the training of skilled labour, provision of better services like transport, banking and communication facilities and so on. All these firms can make use of these facilities, which results in reduction of cost of production.
2. ***Economies of information of technical and market intelligence.*** Each firm in an industry can not have information of technical and market intelligence, R and D, etc., because it costs more to the firms. Hence, when all the firms expand business and all the firms grow, can have only one information centre with all modern facilities through their association to share the services.
3. ***Economies of vertical disintegration.*** With the growth of an industry the firms can not concentrate on all the processes. They can allow some firms to have some specialised processing units to bring specialisation and efficiency in production (outsourcing of some products) which can reduce the cost. This helps some more firms to grow as subsidiaries or auxiliary units. For instance the Automobile industry helps the growth of tyre industry, spare parts firms like electrical, fiber and so on.
4. ***Economies of by products.*** When an industry grows, the waste of one firm will be used by another firm or the same firms as a raw material to produce another product whose value will be comparatively lesser than main products. The revenue derived from this product will reduce the cost of the main product.

Diseconomies of Large Scale Production

When the production of a firm grows in large scale, after a particular stage because of more number of employees, more investment, more production and products the internal and external diseconomies will start to operate. This diseconomy will increases the cost of production and retards the further expansion of the firm. The following are the factors, which leads to diseconomies.

Diseconomies of large scale production
1. Difficulties of management
2. Difficulty in co-ordination
3. Difficulty in decision-making
4. Increased risks

5. Labour diseconomies
6. Scarcity of factors supplies
7. Financial difficulties
8. Marketing diseconomies

1. ***Difficulties of management.*** When the firm expands after a certain point it is very difficult to supervise the production, products, and employees. Hence the diseconomies will operate in the firm. Hence the cost of manufacturing and efficiency in production are effected.
2. ***Difficulty in co-ordination.*** When the firm grows in size, the division of labour and specialization in labour increases. Then the firm appoints various top executives to supervise the activities like marketing, finance, accounts, production, personnel etc. This specialization definitely increases the production and economies of production but after a certain point of its growth co-ordination among all these executives becomes difficult hence it leads to misunderstanding, and hiccups in co-ordination to achieve objectives etc. Hence the cost of production starts increasing.
3. ***Difficulty in decision-making.*** When the size of a firm expands after some point of growth and because of lack of co-ordination among the executives in the organisation consensus becomes difficult. Each executive would of the opinion that his ideas must be considered while decision making. Such biased opinions may hamper the growth of the organisation.
4. ***Increased risks.*** When the firm expands its production and its lines of business naturally the investments will be more. A small mistake in decision making may cause more loss to the organisation.
5. ***Labour diseconomies.*** With the growth of production and specialisation of production, lack of initiative and working zeal among the workers in the organisation may set in, this in turn results in strikes and lockouts, industrial disputes etc.
6. ***Scarcity of factors supplies (localization of firms).*** When all the firms in an industry expanded are then the scarcity of factors of production will arise in that area. This increases the prices of all factors of production and naturally the cost of production.
7. ***Financial difficulties.*** When the firm expands, the problem in raising sufficient funds for their management naturally increases and also proper utilisation of these funds may cause a problem of increase in the cost of capital and affects profits of the firm.
8. ***Marketing diseconomies.*** When the industry expands competition firms will compete with each other to capture the market. In the Monopolistic markets competition, the firms may have to spend huge amount on the promotion and advertisement of their product.

QUESTIONS ON THE CHAPTER

(Two marks)

1. What is Supply? How it is different from stock.
2. Distinguish between supply and stock.

3. What is meant by production function?
4. What are Iso-quants?
5. What is Iso-cost?
6. Give the Iso-product map.
7. Why it is called the law of variable proportions ?
8. What does economies of large-scale production mean?
9. What is meant by internal economies?

(Five marks)

1. Explain the factors determining the supply.
2. When the law of supply does not apply? Explain.
3. Explain the equilibrium of production through the Iso-quant and Iso-cost curves.
4. What is meant by external economies? Explain the various external economies of a firm.

(Fifteen Marks)

1. Explain the law of supply.
2. Explain the law of variable proportions. As a rational producer which of these stage will you choose to operate?
3. What do you mean by internal and external economies? Explain various forms of internal and external economies.
4. Define, classify and explain the economies of large-scale production.
5. Distinguish between internal and external economies. Explain the various internal economies available to a large firm.
6. Describe the law of variable proportions and explain its practical importance in production.
7. Discuss the law of variable proportions with the help of a suitable illustration.

SKILL DEVELOPMENT

1. Write a diagrammatic representation of law of supply.
2. Mention the products for which supply cannot be increased with the increase in the price of a product in our day to day life.
3. List out the products which have elastic and inelastic supply.
4. Give some hypothetical examples to show products equilibrium with the help of law of variable proportion.
5. Draw Iso-quants and Iso-cost curves with examples.
6. From your observation prepare a list of examples for each of the internal economies and external economies of a firm.

CHAPTER

6

COST AND REVENUE ANALYSIS

CHAPTER OUTLINE

Cost

- Concepts
- Short-run costs
- Long-run costs
- Behaviour of different costs TFC, TVC, TC, AFC, AVC, AC and MC
- Relationship between LAC and LMC

Revenue

- Total revenue, Average revenue and Marginal revenue

Problems

- On cost analysis

LEARNING OBJECTIVES

After reading this chapter, you should be able to :

1. Understand the meaning of cost and its behaviour
2. Differentiate between short-run and long-run costs
3. Differentiate between fixed factor and variable factor
4. Recognise different cost concepts
5. Know all about revenue concepts
6. Identify TR, AR and MR
7. Calculate TFC, TVC, TC, AFC, AVC, AC and MC

COST ANALYSIS

The cost analysis plays a very important role in business economics while taking day to day decisions. The information of cost is very important to the management not only to fix the price of a product but also to make strategies to reduce and control the cost of the product. In developing economies like India price is more important than the quality. The multinational T.V manufacturing companies like Thomson, Sony and others including some FMCG manufacturing companies entered the Indian market scene anticipating heavy demand for their quality product, but they failed in their attempt though the population is more. Ultimately they realised that the Indian market is price sensitive rather than quality alone. This lead to reduction in the prices of their products. This reduction in price is possible through the process of cost reduction and control. The reduction of cost and cost control is possible through proper classification of cost like controllable costs and uncontrollable costs, fixed and variable costs, opportunities cost and sunk cost and the like. A study of cost concepts and the cost behaviour is essential for business houses for devising strategies to achieve cost reduction and to fix reasonable price of the products to match the living standards of the people.

Cost Concepts

Before attempting to look at different concepts of cost, it is necessary to understand as to what is cost? Cost is the expenses incurred for the manufacture of a given product. For instance in the manufacture of furniture the expenses like materials, wages for carpenter, and other expenses like fevical, nails, and so on constitute cost of furniture.

There are different concepts of cost like money cost, real cost, opportunity cost and the like. The details are

1. **Money cost of production.** Money cost of production is very important which implies that the aggregate money expenditure incurred by a firm on various factors like rent, wages, salaries to labour, purchase of raw-materials, electrical charges, insurance premium, taxes to the government and so on will enter into the production of a commodity. Money cost is therefore the payment made for the factors in terms of money. It is also known as *nominal cost.*

   The money cost is to be analysed under two time periods, the short period and long period. In the short period, the factors employed by a firm can be divided into two groups, (*a*) Fixed factors and (*b*) Variable factors

   (*a*) ***Fixed factors.*** The factors which cannot be changed or varied irrespective of a rise or fall in the level of output are called Fixed factors. For example: machinery, equipment, rent of the factory building, salaries to permanent staff and the like. The cost incurred on these factors is known as overhead costs, indirect costs or general costs or supplementary costs.

   (*b*) ***Variable factors.*** Factors which do not remain constant, but can be varied in accordance with the changes in the level of output which referred to as Variable factors. Higher the output more will be the variable cost and vice-versa, for example raw materials, electricity, transport, wages to casual labourers and the like. The cost incurred on these factors is known as variable cost. These costs are also otherwise called as the Prime cost, Direct cost or Special cost. The fixed costs and variable costs give the total cost of production (TC).

$$TC = FC + VC$$

2. **Real cost of production.** The term real cost of production is a subjective cost, it expresses the trouble, toil and sacrifices of the factor or its owner. According to marshall "The exertions of all the different kinds of labour that are directly or indirectly involved in making it together with the abstinence or rather the waitings required for savings, the capital used in making it. All these efforts and sacrifices together with, will be called real cost of production of the commodity".

3. **Opportunity cost of production.** Let us understand the meaning of the term opportunity cost by an example. Suppose a manufacturer of Maruti Udyog has Rs five lakh. By using this amount either he can manufacture two 'Maruti 800' cars or one Mauthi Esteem car. If he desires to manufacture the Maruthi 800, he has to sacrifice the opportunity of making the Maruti Esteem with the same amount. This in economics we call opportunity cost or 'sacrified cost' or 'foregone cost'. With limited resources, we have plenty of opportunities to manufacture a number of goods or rendering of services, but we are selecting one opportunity and ignoring the rest and that is opportunity cost. We must weigh each opportunity or alternative on the basis of cost-benefit analysis.

   The concept of opportunity cost is used by the modern economists in modern economic analysis. The principle of opportunity cost in the modern sense is not the pain or strain involved, not the money cost involved in producing a commodity. It depends on the sacrifices of opportunities or alternative products that could be produced instead by using the same factors or by an equivalent group of factors or costing the same amount of money. Thus the opportunity cost of any commodity is the next best alternative goods that is sacrificed.

   This has been explained as follows:

   It is evident that an individual cannot satisfy all wants since the money income at his disposal is limited. Therefore he has to adopt a method of pick and choose between one thing to another.

4. **Explicit cost.** Explicit costs are those costs of production, which are paid by the employer to the owner of factors of production, which do not belong to employer himself. The payment of rent for factory building, interest on capital, purchase of raw-materials, electricity and fuel charges and the like are called explicit cost of production.

5. **Implicit cost.** Implicit cost arises when factors of production are owned by the employer himself, for *eg.* Land, Capital etc. There would be no need to pay rent and interest out of his pocket. The two non-expenditure costs depreciation and the normal return on the money capital supplied by the shareholders will have to be included in this category.

6. **Incremental cost.** Incremental cost refers to the additional cost incurred due to a change in the level or nature of activity like diversification, change in the distribution channel, addition of new machines, going for global businesses and so on. Incremental costs are also known as "differential costs".

7. **Sunk costs.** Sunk costs are those costs which remain unaltered even after a change in the level or nature of activity. These costs are also known as "specific costs". The best example for sunk cost is depreciation. Sunk costs are expenditures that have been made in the past or that must be paid in the future as part of a contractual agreement. The sunk costs are of little or no importance in decision making.

Cost Behaviour

The attempt is made to study the behaviour of cost in relation to the change in output. It is a natural phenomenon that the total cost increases with the increase in output and decreases with the decrease in output. But among the components of total cost the fixed cost remains constant. The variable cost varies in proportion to the change in the output in short run. Whereas in the long run the behaviour of fixed cost is different and it also varies. Hence in long run both fixed and variable costs are variable costs. Similarly the behaviour of average costs also varies with change in the selected period. This chapter focusses on the details of the behaviour of costs and average costs. A sound knowledge of the behaviour of costs and average costs is of paramount importance for the production and finance managers for decision making.

SHORT RUN COST CURVES

Nature and Behaviour of Total Cost, Total Fixed Cost and Total Variable Cost

In the short period there are certain factors of production which remain constant. Their supply is fixed even if the employer wishes to increase. The cost which does not vary with changes in the output is known as Fixed Cost (FC). The rent for factory building, expenditure on capital equipment, specialised human resources, salaries to permanent staff and the like remain unchanged. The fixed costs are also known as supplementary costs, overhead cost or indirect cost.

Variable Costs (VC) are those costs which will vary in accordance with changes in the level of output. A firm can increase the variable costs by employing larger quantities of raw materials, by paying more power charges, excise duties and so on. It is also known as special cost or direct cost.

The Total Cost (TC) is a combination of both total fixed cost and total variable cost *i.e.*, TC = TFC + TVC. The total cost increases as the level of output raises. At zero level of output the firms, fixed cost is equal to its total cost. When output is nil, variable cost is zero. This is explained in the following Fig. 6.1.

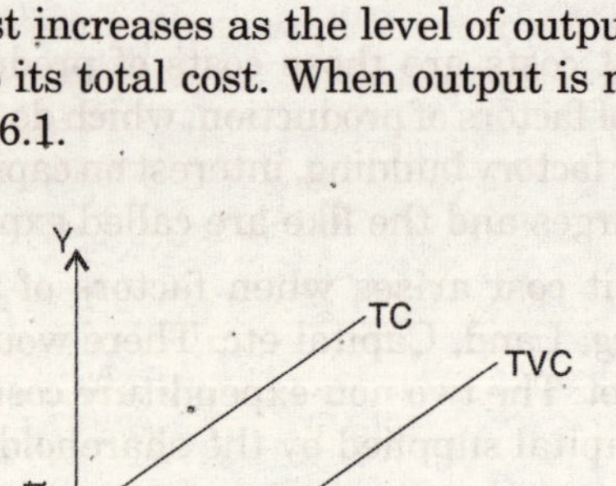

Fig. 6.1. Nature and behaviour of TFC, TVC and TC in short period.

In the Fig. 6.1 on the OX axis the level of output and on the OY axis, the cost are represented. The TFC is a total fixed cost curve, which is a horizontal straight line and parallel to OX axis. It indicates that total fixed cost is incurred even if the output is zero and which remains same whatever may be the output. The TVC is a total variable cost curve which slopes upward from left to right, and starts rising only with the increase in output.

The TC is a total cost curve which increases due to an increase in total variable cost. The total variable cost starts from the origin 'O' which indicates that the variable costs are nil if the output is zero. The total cost is the addition of total fixed cost and total variable cost. It may be noted that in the Fig. 6.1. the vertical distance between total variable cost and total cost curve is constant throughout. This phenomenon is due to the fact that the variable cost and total cost curves represent the amounts of total fixed cost that remains constant, irrespective of a rise or fall in the level of output in the short period.

Nature and Behavior of Average Fixed Cost (AFC), Average Variable Cost (AVC), Average Cost (AC) and Marginal Cost (MC) in Short Run

Average fixed cost is total fixed cost divided by the number of units of output produced. Thus AFC = TFC/ Q where 'Q' is the number of units of output produced. Since the total fixed cost remains constant, the average fixed cost falls continuously as output rises. Çonsequently the average fixed cost curve slops downward from left to right.

Average variable cost is total variable cost divided by the number of units of output produced. Thus AVC = TVC/Q. The average variable cost refers to the cost per unit of output. The average variable cost will be generally 'U' shaped. It will fall as the output increases from zero to normal capacity output due to the operation of increasing return.

Average cost (AC) is the total cost divided by the number of units of output produced. Thus AC = TC/Q. In other words, it is the sum of average fixed cost and average variable cost ie, AC = AFC+AVC. The behaviour of average cost depends upon the behaviour of average fixed cost and average variable cost.

Marginal cost (MC) is the addition made to the total cost It is the extra or additional cost incurred for the production of one more unit of output. Symbolically MCN = TCN – TCN1 that is the marginal cost of Nth unit of output is the total cost of producing 'N' units minus the total cost of producing the previous units of output.

The relation between AFC, AVC, AC and MC is explained in the Fig. 6.2

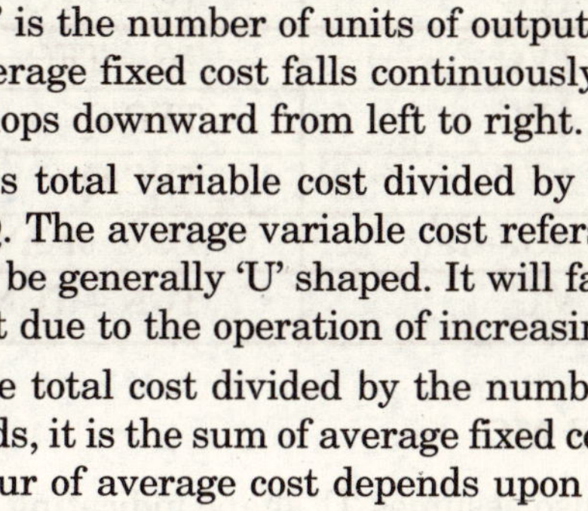

Fig. 6.2. Relationship between AFC, AVC AC and MC.

In the above diagram on the OX axis the level of output and cost on OY axis are represented. In the Fig. 6.2, it is noticeable that the average fixed cost falls as output increases from lower levels to higher levels. The average fixed cost curve slopes downward from left to right. Since the TFC remains constant, the AFC progressively diminishes with every increase in output. The average variable cost curve first falls and then rises. The AVC is slightly 'U' shaped indicating that as the output increases, initially, the AVC declines, then it remains constant for a while and again starts increasing.

The behaviour of average cost depends upon the behaviour of AFC and AVC curves. In the beginning both AFC and AVC falls and hence the AC also falls. As output increases, AFC decreases and AC also falls, but the AVC curve tends to rise sharply this is due to the operation of the law of diminishing returns (Diseconomies of production). Therefore, the AC rises after a point. The AC like AVC falls first, reaches the minimum point and then rises. Hence, it is assumed that the AC is 'U' shaped in the short period.

Cost Equations

Cost	Equation
TC	TC = TFC + TVC
TFC	TC – TVC
TVC	TC – TFC
AFC	TFC/Q
AVC	TVC/Q
AC	TC/Q or AVC + AVC
MC	TCN – TCN1

Relationship between AC and MC

The marginal cost curve also assumes 'U' shape indicating that in the beginning the MC declines as output rises, thereafter, it remains constant for a while then starts rising. The MC curve intersects both the AVC curve and the AC curve at their minimum points. *Minimum point* is a point at which the average cost curve is about to increase. In the short-run the MC is directly related to variable cost, and the shape of the MC curve is determined by the law of variable proportion.

Long-run Average Cost

In the long period all costs become variable costs and there are no fixed costs. The long run average costs are generally 'U' shaped just like the short-run average curves. The only difference is that they are much flatter than the short-run cost curves. In other words, the long run cost curves are less pronounced and 'U' shaped, the reason for which may be explained in terms of fixed costs and variable costs. It should be noted that fixed costs do not possess the same importance in the long as well as in the short-run. In fact in the long period fixed factors become variable factors, because the time period is long enough to vary the firms fixed factor inputs.

The long run average cost curve is indicated in the diagram.

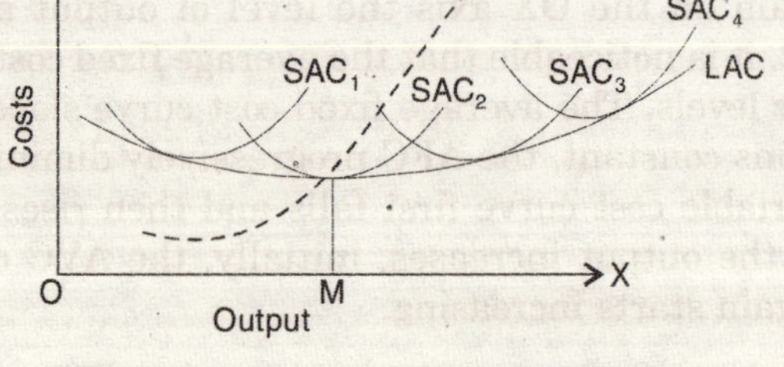

Fig. 6.3. Long-run average cost curve.

The long-run average cost is derived as the tangent to the various short-run average cost curves. The size of the plant is determined by the shape of the curve and in the long-run a rational entrepreneur would select the optimum scale of output. It is that size of output at which short run average cost is tangent to long-run average cost, at that point both the curves have the minimum point of tangency. In the Fig. 6.3 at OM level of output SAC^2 is tangent to LAC. Thus OM is regarded as the optimum scale of output. The long run average cost curve is sometimes called as the normal cost or the planning curve. It also helps the entrepreneur to plan his course of action in the long run and it can make adjustments in the long-run to reduce the cost per unit. The long run cost curve is the family of various short run cost curves appropriate to different levels of output. Therefore, it is also called as ***'Envelope curve'***.

Relationship between Long-run Marginal Cost and Long-run Average Cost

Like the short run marginal costs curve, the long run marginal cost curve is also derived from the slope of the total cost curve at various points relating to the given output each time.

The behaviour of LMC is shown in the Fig. 6.4

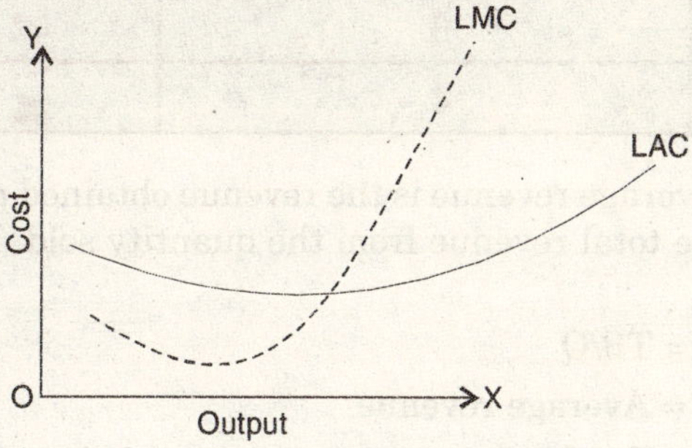

Fig. 6.4

In the Fig. 6.4, (1) both MC and AC curves are sloping down ward, when LAC also falls and LMC is lesser than LAC.

(2) When LAC is the minimum, LMC is equal to LAC. Thus, the LMC intersects LAC at the lower point.

(3) When LMC is rising, LAC also rises faster than LAC, at this point LMC > LAC.

REVENUE ANALYSIS

The study of revenue analysis is important to the managers of the organisation similar to cost analysis. The profitability of the organisation depends not only on the cost analysis but also revenue analysis. The revenue analysis guides the management to determine the price of a commodity or service. In the competitive and imperfect markets such as monopoly, duopoly, oligopoly and monopolistic competition the price is determined by the use of revenue analysis or revenue curves like average revenue and marginal revenue. Hence there is a need to understand some of the revenue concepts for better and simple diagnosis of the revenue gamut of a company.

Revenue. The term revenue refers to the amount obtained from the sale of goods or services. In simple words, revenue means income or receipts obtained from the selling of goods or services.

Total revenue. It refers to the sum of income or receipts from the sale of all goods at various prices. In other words, total revenue is the product of total units sold multiplied by the price per unit.

Symbolically,

$$TR = P \times Q$$

where TR = Total revenue

Q = Quantity of goods sold

P = Price per unit

The Table 6.1 shows the total revenue.

Table 6.1

Quantity sold	Price per unit (in Rs.)	Total revenue (in Rs.)
100	10	1000
200	8	1600
350	6	2100
600	4	2400

Average revenue. Average revenue is the revenue obtained per unit of commodity sold. It is obtained by dividing the total revenue from the quantity sold. It is called average selling price per unit.

Thus, AR = TR/Q

where AR = Average revenue

TR = Total revenue

Q = Quantity sold

The Table 6.2 shows the total revenue and average revenue

Table 6.2

Quantity sold	Price per unit (in Rs.)	Total revenue (in Rs.)	Average revenue (in Rs)
100	10	1000	10
200	8	1600	8
350	6	2100	6
600	4	2400	4

Marginal revenue. Marginal revenue is the revenue generated by selling one more additional unit. It is also defined as the revenue obtained form the selling of an additional unit. In other words marginal revenue is the change in total revenue per unit with the change in the sale of an additional unit.

The Table 6.3 shows the total revenue, average revenue and marginal revenue

Table 6.3

Quantity sold or AR (in Rs.)	Price per unit (in Rs.)	Total revenue (in Rs)	Marginal revenue
1	10	10	10
2	8	16	6
3	6	18	2
4	4	16	–2
5	3	15	–1
6	2	12	–3

The revenue like total revenue, average revenue and marginal revenue can be represented on the diagram as shown in the Fig. 6.5

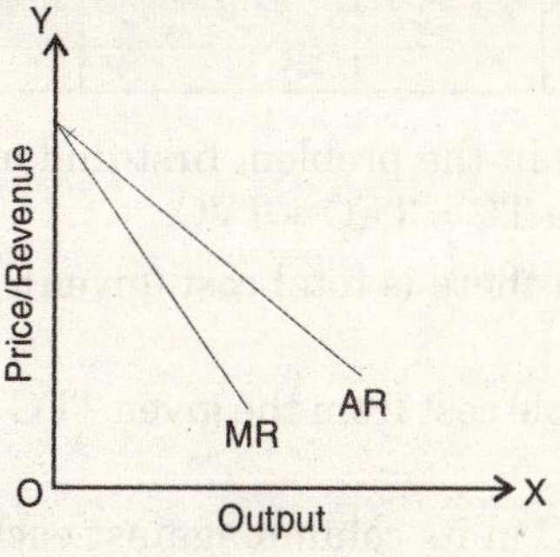

Fig. 6.5. Shows total revenue, average revenue and marginal revenue.

QUESTIONS ON THE CHAPTER

(Two marks)

1. What is meant by opportunity cost?
2. Distinguish between money cost and real cost.
3. What is sunk cost?
4. What is meant by implicit cost? Give an example.
5. Distinguish between fixed cost and variable cost.
6. Distinguish between AFC and AVC.
7. What is meant by average cost?
8. Why LAC curve is called 'envelop curve'?
9. What do you mean by total revenue? How it is arrived.
10. Distinguish between 'average revenue' and 'marginal revenue'
11. Give reason for U-shaped average cost curve.

(Five marks)

1. Explain the behaviour of fixed cost, variable and total cost curves in short run.
2. Explain the behaviour of short run average cost curves.
3. Why the LAC curve is flatter in 'U' shape? Explain
4. Explain the relationship between AC and MC curve in short run.

COST ANALYSIS

Tips to solve the problems on cost analysis

1. The student should adhere to the format given below at the time of solving the problems.

   Format to solve the problems on cost analysis

Output (in units)	*Total fixed cost*	*Total variable cost*	*Total cost*	*Average fixed cost*	*Average variable cost*	*Average cost*	*Marginal cost*

2. If Fixed cost is not given in the problem first find out fixed cost from the given total cost by using the formula TC = TFC + TVC.
3. If the output is zero, and there is total cost (given), the entire total cost is total fixed cost
4. Calculate the total variable cost from the given TFC and TC by using the formulae TC =TFC+TVC.
5. Enter the calculated TFC in its column against each level of output, it is same at all level of output.
6. Calculate the averages of other TFC, TVC and TC to calculate AFC,AVC and AC respectively by using the formulae given in the previous pages.
7. Calculate marginal cost from the changes in the total cost

SOLVED PROBLEMS

1. *From the following data calculate the total variable cost, average fixed cost, average variable cost, average cost and marginal cost.*

Output (in units)	*0*	*1*	*2*	*3*	*4*	*5*	*6*	*7*	*8*
Total cost (in Rs)	*400*	*480*	*550*	*590*	*620*	*650*	*730*	*820*	*950*

Solution.

Hints.

(*a*) When total cost is there at zero output, that cost is total fixed cost *i.e.*, Rs. 400 enter in its column.

(*b*) Calculate total variable cost by deducting total fixed cost from total cost and enter in its column, *i.e.*, TVC = TC – TFC.

(*c*) Now calculate AFC = TFC/output , AVC = TVC/ output or quantity, AC = TC/ quantity

Statement showing TVC, AFC, AVC, AC and MC

Output (in units)	*Total fixed cost*	*Total variable*	*Total cost*	*Average fixed cost*	*Average variable*	*Average cost*	*Marginal cost*
0	400	—	400	400	—	400	–
1	400	80	480	400	80	480	80
2	400	150	550	200	75	275	70
3	400	190	590	133	63.33	196.33	40
4	400	220	620	100	55	155	30
5	400	250	650	80	41.67	121.67	30
6	400	330	730	67	55	122	80
7	400	420	820	57	60	117	90
8	400	550	950	50	68.75	118.75	130

2. *A small firm with a fixed cost of Rs. 20. The total variable cost for the successive quantities of output per day are as follows:*

Output (in units)	*1*	*2*	*3*	*4*	*5*	*6*	*7*
Total variable cost (in Rs)	*30*	*56*	*75*	*80*	*105*	*132*	*182*

Find the total cost, average fixed cost, average variable cost, average cost and marginal cost of the firm for each level of output.

Solution

Hints.

(*a*) TFC is given in the problem, enter this in the TFC column.

(*b*) Enter total variable cost in its column from the given problem.

(*c*) Calculate T C by adding TFC and TVC.

(*d*) Now calculate AFC, AVC, AC and MC.

Statement showing TC, AFC, AVC, AC and MC

Output (in units)	*Total fixed cost*	*Total variable cost*	*Total cost*	*Average fixed cost*	*Average variable cost*	*Average cost*	*Marginal cost*
1	20	30	50	20	30	50	–
2	20	56	76	10	28	38	6
3	20	75	95	6.67	25	31.67	19
4	20	80	100	5	20	27	5
5	20	105	125	4	21	24	25
6	20	132	152	3.33	22	25.33	27
7	20	182	202	2.85	26	28.85	50

3. *With the help of the data given below, find out (1) Total fixed cost; (2) Total Variable cost; (3) Total cost; (4) Average fixed cost; (5) Average cost; and (6) Marginal cost of the firm.*

Units of output	*Average fixed cost Rs.*	*Average variable cost. Rs.*
0	—	—
1	—	10
2	—	9
3	—	8
4	—	8
5	—	10
6	5	12

Solution.

Hints to work out the problem.

(*a*) Calculate total fixed cost from average fixed cost given at the out put of 6 units. TFC= AFC × Out put at that level. *i.e.,* 5 × 6 units = 30 and now enter in its column.

(*b*) Find out TVC from AVC at each level of output by multiplying AVC with concerned output.

(*c*) Now find out TC. I., TFC + TVC = TC and enter in its column.

(*d*) Find out the AFC, AC and MC.

(*e*) Calculate marginal cost from the changes in the total cost with the change in output.

Statement showing TC, AFC, AVC, AC and MC

Output (in units)	*Total fixed cost*	*Total variable cost*	*Total cost*	*Average fixed cost*	*Average variable cost*	*Average cost*	*Marginal cost*
0	30	—	30	30	—	30	30
1	30	10	40	30	10	40	10
2	30	18	48	15	9	24	8
3	30	24	54	10	8	18	6
4	30	32	62	7.5	8	15.5	8
5	30	50	80	6	10	16	18
6	30	72	102	5	12	17	22

4. *A Manufacturing concern incurs a total fixed cost of Rs. 120. With the help of the information given below calculate:*

(*i*) *Total variable cost*
(*ii*) *Total cost*
(*iii*) *Average fixed cost*
(*iv*) *Average variable cost*
(*v*) *Average cost*

Output (in units)	*0*	*1*	*2*	*3*	*4*	*5*	*6*
Marginal cost (in Rs)	—	*60*	*20*	*10*	*15*	*35*	*70*

Solution.

Hints to solve the problem

(*a*) First enter the fixed cost in its column at all level of output

(*b*) Calculate total cost from the marginal cost. Calculate total cost by adding marginal cost *i.e.,* at zero output total cost is Rs. 120 because there is no total variable cost. At the output of one unit total cost is 120 of previous output plus marginal cost *i.e.,* 180. At units of output the total cost is previous output total cost plus marginal cost of this unit *i.e.,* 180 + 20 = 200 and so on.

(*c*) Now calculate total variable cost by deducting total fixed cost from total cost.

Statement showing TVC, TC, AFC, AVC, AC and MC

Output (in units)	*Total fixed cost*	*Total variable cost*	*Total cost*	*Average fixed cost*	*Average variable cost*	*Average cost*	*Marginal cost*
0	120	—	120	120	—	120	—
1	120	60	180	120	30	180	60
2	120	80	200	60	40	100	20
3	120	90	210	40	30	70	10
4	120	105	225	30	26.25	56.25	15
5	120	140	260	24	28	52	35
6	120	210	330	20	35	55	70

5. *The fixed cost of a manufacturing concern is Rs. 400. Calculate TVC, TC, AC and AFC from the following.*

Output (in units)	*1*	*2*	*3*	*4*	*5*	*6*
Average variable cost (in Rs)	*60*	*55*	*40*	*65*	*90*	*120*

Solution.

Hints in solving the problem

(*a*) Enter the given TFC in its column.

(*b*) Enter AVC also in its column.

(*c*) Calculate TVC from given AVC by multiplying AVC at each level of output with the number of units manufactured.

(*d*) Now calculate TC by adding both TFC and TVC.

(*e*) Calculate AFC, AC and MC. Now you calculate MC from the total cost. The change in TC with the change in the production of an additional unit.

Statement showing, TVC, TC, AFC, AC and MC

Output (in units)	*Total fixed cost*	*Total variable cost*	*Total cost*	*Average fixed cost*	*Average variable cost*	*Average cost*	*Marginal cost*
1	400	60	460	400	60	460	—
2	400	110	510	200	55	255	50
3	400	120	520	133.33	40	173.33	10
4	400	260	660	100	65	165	140
5	400	450	850	80	90	170	190
6	400	720	1120	66.67	120	186.67	270

6. *From the data given below, calculate total variable cost, average cost and marginal cost. Explain the behaviour of TFC, TVC and TC with the help of graphic illustration.*

Output (in Units)	*0*	*1*	*2*	*3*	*4*	*5*	*6*
Total cost (in Rs)	*360*	*540*	*600*	*630*	*675*	*780*	*990*

Solution.

Statement showing TFC, TVC, TC, AFC, AVC, AC and MC

Output (in units)	*Total fixed cost*	*Total variable cost*	*Total cost*	*Average fixed cost*	*Average variable cost*	*Average cost*	*Marginal cost*
0	360	—	360	360	—	360	—
1	360	180	540	360	180	540	180
2	360	240	600	180	120	300	60
3	360	270	630	120	90	210	30
4	360	315	675	90	78.75	168.75	45
5	360	420	780	72	84	156	105
6	360	630	990	60	105	165	210

The behaviour of TFC, TVC and TC is explained with the help of graph

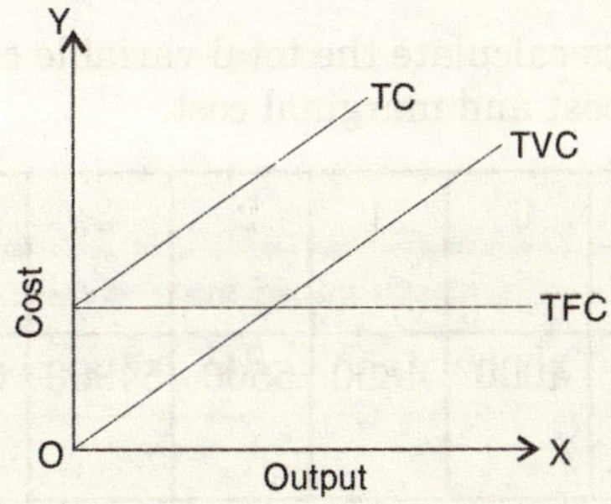

On OX axis output in units is represented. On OY axis the cost is represented. TFC is a horizontal straight line to the OX axis, starts on the OY axis, not from 'O' point because even at zero or 'O' output there are fixed costs. These fixed costs remains constant whatever may be the output, hence it is a horizontal straight line to the OX axis. The TVC curve goes on increasing from 'O' point indicating that the variable costs increases in proportion to the output. The TC is a combination of both TFC and TVC, hence it behaves as that of both. Hence TC curve lies above TVC. The TC curve starts from where the TVC curve starts, because even at zero output there is TC, this is due to existence of TFC.

EXERCISE PROBLEMS

1. With the help of the schedule given below, calculate TFC, TVC, AC, and MC. Give a graphic illustration to explain the relationship between output and total cost.

Output (in units)	0	1	2	3	4	5	6
Total cost (in Rs)	300	400	480	540	620	800	1020

2. A firm gives the following information regarding its cost and output. You are required to calculate AVC, TVC, TC and MC at different levels of output.

Output	*AFC*	*AC*
0		200
1		240
2		130
3		90.66
4		80
5		90
6		98.33
7		108.57
8	25	125

3. Using the following data calculate the total variable cost, average fixed cost, average variable cost, average cost and marginal cost.

Output (in units)	0	1	2	3	4	5	6
Total cost (in Rs)	4000	4800	5500	54900	6200	6500	7300

4. From the following data given below calculate TFC, TVC, TC, AFC, AVC and AC

Output (in units)	0	1	2	3	4	5	6
Marginal cost (in Rs)	360	180	60	30	45	105	110

5. A manufacturing firm incurs a Total Fixed cost of Rs. 120. With the help of the information given below find out :

(*i*) Total variable cost

(*ii*) Total cost

(*iii*) Average fixed cost and

(*iv*) Average cost.

(*v*) Marginal cost

Output (in units)	0	1	2	3	4	5	6
Avearge variable cost (in Rs)	—	20	30	20	16.25	18	25

PROBLEMS ON REVENUE ANALYSIS

1. *With the help of the data given below, calculate average returns and marginal returns. Explain their behaviour with the help of graphic illustration.*

Units of variable factors	*1*	*2*	*3*	*4*	*5*	*6*	*7*
Total output (Quintals)	*20*	*36*	*48*	*56*	*60*	*60*	*56*

Solution.

Statement showing the calculation of AR and MR

Units of variable factors	*Total output (Quintals) (TR)*	*Average Returns (AR = TR/output)*	*Marginal Returns*
1	20	20	—
2	36	18	16
3	48	16	12
4	56	14	8
5	60	12	4
6	60	10	0
7	56	8	–4

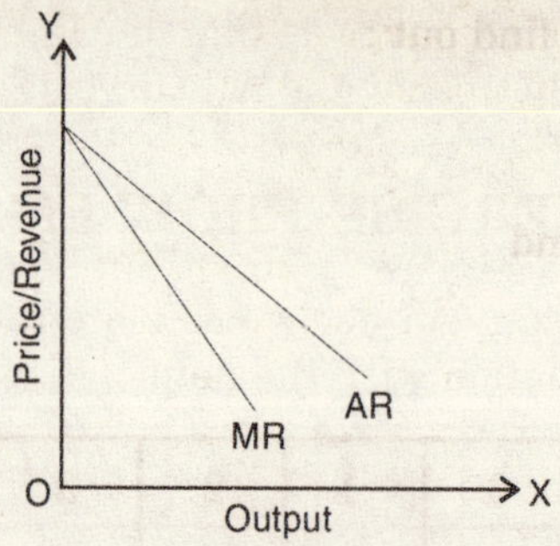

Behaviour

(*a*) The total revenue or output first increases with the increase in variable factors after some point it starts decreasing, this is because of the law of returns.

(*b*) The average return goes on decreasing with every additional unit of variable factors, hence the AR curve slopes downward from right to left.

(*c*) The marginal revenue also behaves as that of AR, but this is always lesser than AR. Therefore the MR curve lies below the AR curve.

2. *With the help of the data given below calculate the average returns and marginal returns. Explain their relation with the help of diagram.*

Units of variable factors	*1*	*2*	*3*	*4*	*5*	*6*	*7*	*8*
Total output (in units)	*100*	*180*	*240*	*280*	*300*	*300*	*280*	*240*

Solution .

Statement showing the calculation of AR and MR

Units of variable factors	*Total output (Quintals) (TR)*	*Average returns (AR = TR/output)*	*Marginal returns*
1	100	100	—
2	180	90	20
3	240	80	60
4	280	70	40
5	300	60	20
6	300	50	0
7	280	40	– 20
8	240	30	– 40

Behaviour

(*d*) The total revenue or output first increases with the increase in variable factors after some point it starts decreasing, this is because of the law of returns.

(*e*) The average return goes on decreasing with every additional unit of variable factors, hence the AR curve slopes downward from right to left.

(*f*) The marginal revenue also behaves as that of AR, but this is always lesser than AR. Therefore the MR curve lies below the AR curve. (See Fig. 6.5)

EXERCISE PROBLEMS

1. With the help of the data given below calculate the average returns and marginal returns. Explain their relation with the help of diagram.

Units of variable factors	1	2	3	4	5	6	7
Total returns (in units)	1000	1800	2400	2800	3000	3000	2800

SKILL DEVELOPMENT

1. Collect profit and loss account of a sole trader from your neighborhood (SSI) and identify which are explicit costs and implicit costs from it.

2. Construct a diagram showing cost behavior of fixed cost curve, variable cost curve and total cost curve in the short run.

3. Prepare a diagram showing the behaviour of AFC, AVC, AC and MC.

4. Prepare a diagram showing the behavior of SAC, and MC curve.

5. Two of your B.Com students decide to open a business, and all the two devote their full time to its management. What cost would you assign to their time? Is this an explicit or implicit cost?

6. The agreement to pay warehouse rent of Rs. 500 per month. It is an example for explicit cost or sunk cost.

CASE STUDY

Rakesh is a student of commerce. Since he joined commerce stream in Pre-university, he kept the record of the amount spent on studying the course. Similarly he collected the amount spent by his friends who joined science and switched over to Engineering, Medicine, Bio-tech and so on. Then he arrived at the amount spent by each one of them. He also calculated what would be the amount if the same would have been invested in some financial instruments like recurring deposit, equity shares, or in the enterprise of their own. Then he arrived at what is the opportunity cost for their investments in these two alternatives. Similarly assume that your investment in studies is Rs. 1 lakh and find out the alternatives amount of money you get it from the above said opportunities and find the opportunity whether you have foregone by investing in degree course.

Answer the following:

1. What Rakesh has to do?

2. Can you identify the opportunity cost involved in the above case?

3. Whether Mr. Rakesh is going for investment in financial products or in education?

4. Which according to you is the eternal asset? Why? Justify your answer.

5. If you were to be in Rakesh's position, would you strike a balance between investment in financial products and education? (By applying ***"Earn while you Learn"*** principle).